Toolbox
for [Busy] Pastors

BARRY CAMPBELL

Convention Press
Nashville, Tennessee

LifeWay Church Resources
a division of LifeWay Christian Resources
of the Southern Baptist Convention
One LifeWay Plaza
Nashville, Tennessee 37234

Dedication

This resource is dedicated to J. Walker Campbell and Bill Davie. Walker Campbell was my earthly father and my father in the ministry. Bill Davie was the father of my precious wife Marci and a wise counselor to me for almost two decades. These two men walked so patiently with me that I cannot imagine my ministry without them. Among the many benefits of having these two spiritual giants in my life was the practical help they gave me as I made my way through those first few years of my ministry. Their wisdom and experience perfectly counterbalanced my inexperience. I thank God for sending these two men into my life and pray that God will send some Paul into the life of every young Timothy.

Acknowledgments

I appreciate very much the many people who have impacted this resource. Some have actually researched and written articles that have been included in *Toolbox*. My coworkers here at LifeWay Christian Resources, including Tommy Yessick, John Garner, Gary Aylor and his fine team in the Stewardship Department, and Dean Richardson all provided excellent written resources. Jerry Barlow and Perry Hancock of New Orleans Baptist Theological Seminary wrote practical and helpful pieces that are included. All these have worked with excellence to produce the very best and most helpful resource possible.

Toolbox is a how-to resource intended to provide quick help on lots of subjects. In many cases, more comprehensive work has been done on that subject. Many pastors will benefit from accessing the more exhaustive treatments referenced in *Toolbox*.

A special word of appreciation is due Judi Hayes, the editor of *Toolbox*. Her encouragement and attention to detail made working on this resource a joy.

Contents

Preface

Welcome to *Toolbox for Busy Pastors*.

This resource is designed to provide practical help for pastors. It is our prayer that each brief article will give you a useful step-by-step process or a few helpful ideas.

Not much time is devoted to philosophical groundwork. In fact, this resource assumes that the pastor has a strong biblical foundation. Every effort has been made to use the limited space available to provide the most practical, how-to help possible. In the article on outreach, for example, little time is spent in an effort to convince pastors to do outreach. Instead, the article goes directly to the meat of how to develop a 12-month plan.

Several kinds of input have gone into this resource. Most of the articles are simply based on my personal experience and that of those who mentored me. I was privileged to serve as a pastor for 18 years. My father, Walker Campbell, was a pastor for 40 years; and my wife's father, Bill Davie, served as a pastor for more than 40 years. Both my father and my father-in-law were wonderful pastors, and their influence in my life has been immeasurable.

Some articles are based on ideas gathered during my years of travel as a LifeWay Church Resources consultant. Meeting pastors from all around the country has provided the opportunity to share ideas with some gifted leaders. In some cases, I researched a subject and combined that information with other input. In a few articles, I simply adapted an existing work to fit the format of this document. In all cases, I have done my best to credit authors and originators.

It is a great joy and privilege to serve God as a pastor. May this resource help pastors use their time and energy in the best way. God bless you as you continue to serve Him.

1. ⬤HOW TO Lead Your Church to Grow

In *Kingdom Principles for Church Growth*, Gene Mims said there are five things every church should do. These functions are evangelism, discipleship, fellowship, ministry, and worship. When these five things are done in a healthy and balanced manner, church growth will be the natural result.

Church growth is natural. It is natural for living things to grow to maturity. When they don't grow, something is wrong. It is natural for the church to grow. If your church isn't growing, something is wrong. Church growth is achieved by doing natural things in a healthy, balanced manner.

To lead your church to grow, do something intentional about each of these five functions.

Evangelism.—Don't neglect the basics. In *Effective Evangelistic Churches*, Tom Rainer told about his research into what more than five hundred evangelistic churches are doing to fulfill the Great Commission. It surprised some to learn that most evangelistic churches are doing some pretty basic, even traditional things. They do weekly outreach. They have revivals. They have strong Sunday Schools.

Be intentional. Plan an outreach project each quarter. Include witness training, prospect discovery, and projects designed to encourage your people to participate in outreach.

Lead your church to participate in an evangelism process. FAITH is a process of doing evangelism through the Sunday School. *Outreach Teams That Win: Grow* is a way to organize your church into four outreach teams. Find a ministry that matches your church and get involved.

Be a personal soul-winner. If you, personally, are faithful to share your faith with others, your church will baptize many each year.

Discipleship.—Make Sunday School a priority. Start a new Bible Study group. Enlist your teachers and provide training for them. Fulfill the Great Commission through your Sunday School.

Encourage your people to involve themselves personally in discipling others. Any time one believer engages another and the result is that they are both more like Christ, discipleship is happening. Whether two neighbors share a cup of coffee as they study the Bible or a group meets for Bible study in an apartment complex, encourage your people to disciple others.

9

Fellowship.—Fellowship is more than punch and cookies. When we bear one another's burdens, fellowship is strong. When we rejoice in the common blessings we share as Christians, that is fellowship.

Encourage Sunday School classes to be intentional about fellowship. One strong Sunday School class gathers to share a meal once a month. This fellowship time around a meal opens the door for class members to bear one another's burdens.

Make much of the fellowship of the Lord's Supper. This is a time of fellowship and worship. The Lord's Supper shows us and the world all that we have in common in the body and blood of Jesus.

Ministry.—No matter how many people you win, your church will not grow without effective ministry. Organize your Sunday School to minister. The Sunday School class I attend has 15 members. Because of the relatively small group, we are able to keep up with ministry needs. Every Sunday School class should be organized to meet needs in Jesus name.

Involve your deacons in ministry. The Deacon Family Ministry Plan is used effectively by many congregations.

Worship.—Worship can be defined as an encounter with God. While one may encounter God in many places, that encounter should always take place when the church is gathered on the Lord's Day.

Strive for excellence. You would not dare enter the pulpit without praying and preparing extensively for the sermon you will deliver. The same attention should be given the rest of the worship experience. Pray, prepare, and make the Lord's day the most warm, authentic worship experience possible.

Resources

Mims, Gene. *Kingdom Principles for Church Growth,* revised and expanded. Nashville: LifeWay Press, 2001.

Rainer, Tom. S. *Effective Evangelistic Churches.* Nashville: Broadman & Holman, 1996.

Tidwell, Jerry N. *Outreach Teams That Win: G.R.O.W.* Nashville: Convention Press, 1998.

2. (HOW TO) Understand Who You Are as a Leader

Who you are as a leader is impacted by lots of outside forces. Certainly, a clear, strong call from God to serve Him as a pastor has great impact. Also, people you encounter as you prepare and serve are significant. Books and other resources help to shape us. And the natural and spiritual gifts God has given us have a great part in making us the leaders we are. Here are a few tips that may help you understand who you are as a leader. In *Kingdom Leadership*, Mike Miller identified six steps on a Leadership Path.

Beginning Leader

All of us have been through this beginning level of leadership, and most of us have returned there from time to time. This is a time of gathering the tools to use later in your ministry. The beginning leader might be young but might also be an experienced person who is beginning some new kind of ministry. Even while the beginning leader is learning, significant ministry should be taking place.

Assimilating Leader

This is the place on the Leadership Path where a leader continues to acquire leadership tools and further develop the leadership tools already being practiced. Just as a warrior needs an array of weapons from which to choose, the effective leader needs a toolbox full of leadership skills.

Building Leader

The building leader is at that time in ministry when more emphasis is on doing ministry than preparing for ministry. This is not to suggest that no more beginning or assimilating is needed. In fact, we all return to those first levels frequently. Every time a leader begins a new ministry, moves to a new church field, or simply enters a new chapter in life, in a sense the leader is once again a beginner. The building leader takes those tools that have been gathered and builds something with them.

Achieving Leader

This leader has taken a step beyond simply building something with leadership tools. He is doing that which God called and equipped him as a leader to do. Achievement is not a measure of the size of a church or the length of time in ministry. Becoming an achieving leader means the leader is doing what God has prepared him to do. Success is found in faithfulness.

Maturing Leader

This level of leadership is more than just surviving to maturity in years or tenure. It should be a time when the leader has gathered enough leadership tools and experience to consider becoming a mentor for a younger or more inexperienced leader. It is a time of sharing and should be a time of celebrating all that God has done through that leader. The maturing leader may be entering some of his most productive years in the kingdom.

Refocusing Leader

The refocusing leader is not ready to stop serving God as a kingdom leader. Instead, he is ready for a new focus or a new direction in ministry. This pastor may or may not continue active service as pastor of a local church. Many faithful pastors serve in that capacity well beyond the traditional age of retirement, and they do so with excellence. Others change the focus of their ministry and continue to serve God with faithfulness and excellence in some capacity other than local-church pastor. Some continue to serve as pastors but do so in another place, such as the mission field or some part of the country where an experienced pastor with a retirement income would be most welcome.

Where are you on the Leadership Path? Remember, the path is not a linear process in which a leader marches directly from one level to the next without ever retracing his steps. An effective leader will find himself a beginner many times during his ministry. Study the path; determine which level, or levels, describe you; and use that information to guide your personal development as a leader.

Resource

Miller, Mike. *Kingdom Leadership: A Call to Christ-Centered Leadership*.
    Nashville: Convention Press, 1996.

12

3. (HOW TO) Understand Which Leadership Style Is Best for You

Every year thousands of pastors go to a convention or conference and hear a wonderful leader describe his leadership style. He is indeed a forceful, dynamic leader. He tells of putting antagonists in their places with nerves of steel and tremendous confidence.

I really do appreciate those forceful, dynamic leaders who seem always to walk ahead of the crowd and overcome opposition by the sheer force of their strong personalities. They are a gift from God, and God uses their leadership to further His kingdom. But not every pastor is gifted to be that kind of leader.

The results can be tragic when leaders try to put on a leadership style that does not fit. They seem awkward and uncertain. Worse yet, these leaders miss the real potential of using their own God-given gifts to become the most effective leaders possible.

Rather than attempting to become something they are not, pastors would do well to think of leadership styles as tools to be used when appropriate. Every pastor needs to pick up different leadership tools for different situations and with different people. Even if you are not gifted to be a directing, almost dictatorial leader, you will, at times, need to pick up directing leadership from your leadership toolbox and use it. This is not hypocritical. You are simply using a tool, not attempting to become a kind of leader you are not gifted or inclined to become. While you should develop the ability to use a certain leadership tool and then put it away until it is needed again, you should also learn to recognize and develop your natural or primary leadership style.

In *The Empowered Leader*, Calvin Miller identified four leadership styles.[1] Many writers and thinkers have described the array of leadership styles or approaches. I have chosen to share Miller's for two reasons. First, he has simplified it to a list of four. While this list is not exhaustive, it is helpful. Second, Miller presented four leadership styles, and all of them are developed as strong, positive approaches to leadership. Some writers develop a list, and the two extremes are undesirable while those in the middle of the list are acceptable.

Here are Miller's leadership styles. You may want to put them in your toolbox.

The Directing Leader

This leader gives specific instructions and supervises closely.

The Coaching Leader

This leader directs and supervises closely but also explains decisions, invites suggestions from the team, and supports progress made by team members. This leadership approach is comfortable for me personally because it allows the pastor to be a strong leader while realizing that he is part of a team. He is the coach but still part of the team.

The Supporting Leader

This leader is a coach, but he goes one step further. The supporting leader also shares authority and decision making with team members. Some people on your team are of sufficient maturity and ability to warrant the sharing of authority and decision making.

The Delegating Leader

This leader actually gives so much authority to team members that he trusts them to make decisions and solve problems without his direct involvement. As a pastor, you are blessed if you have volunteer or paid staff members who can function well under delegating leadership.

As you can see, each of these styles has value. Some people and some situations demand a directing style. Others need a supporting style. Choose to use the style which is appropriate for the person and the situation.

One last thing to remember about which leadership style is best. My son, Jesse, was watching a Christian video one day. As I walked by, one of the characters said, "God gives strength to the humble, but He flattens the hot-shot."[2] That's a pretty good word for a leader. Whatever leadership style you choose, approach it with humility.

Resource

Miller, Calvin. *The Empowered Leader.* Nashville: Broadman & Holman, 1995.

---

[1]Kenneth Blanchard, *The One Minute Manager* (New York: William Morrow and Company, 1985), 30, as referenced in Calvin Miller, *The Empowered Leader* (Nashville: Broadman & Holman, 1995).
[2]*McGee and Me: A Star in the Breaking* (Wheaton, IL: Tyndale Christian Video, 1990).

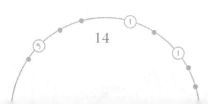

14

4. (HOW TO) Plan Strategically the Work of Your Church

Most church leaders begin their planning at the wrong place. When the time comes to plan, they get out the calendars and calculators and start matching up activities and dates.

In *Kingdom Principles for Church Growth*, Gene Mims pointed out five things every church should do—evangelism, discipleship, fellowship, ministry, and worship. Mims said that when a church practices these five functions in a healthy manner, numerical increase, spiritual growth, missions increase, and ministry advance will follow. Since we know these are the essential functions of the church, it makes sense to plan according to these five functions.

This process is an abbreviated description of *Kingdom Principles Growth Strategies,* by Mike Miller and Gene Mims, a resource that contains simple, easy-to-use instructions for the entire strategic planning process.

Foundation for Planning

Start with the Great Commission, the marching orders of the church.—
As you begin the planning process, teach your people that the church is commanded to reach people for Christ, baptize them, and teach them all the things Jesus taught us.

> ***Teach your people about the Kingdom of God.—***Using *Kingdom Principles for Church Growth*, help your people see the work of the church with a kingdom perspective.
>
> Lead your church to develop and adopt purpose and vision statements. A purpose statement is a contemporary restatement of the Great Commission. A vision statement is about how your church will carry out the Great Commission in its setting. The Leader's Guide in *Kingdom Principles Growth Strategies* contains help for developing these statements. Rick Warren's *The Purpose Driven Church* also contains a helpful process for writing a purpose statement.
>
> ***Discover the spiritual giftedness of your church.—***Using a good spiritual gifts inventory, take a look at the giftedness of your people. LifeWay Church Resources produces a simple, easy-to-use instrument called *Spiritual Gifts Inventory.*
>
> These foundational steps in the planning process are vital. When the time

comes for putting events on the calendar, each potential action should be viewed through the lenses of these first steps. Ask: "Is this activity in line with the kingdom of God and the Great Commission? Does it line up with the purpose of our church?" You may discover that you are investing too much time, energy, and money in activities that have little to do with what your church ought to be doing.

Assessment for Planning

The process is called SWOTs. Assess the strengths, weaknesses, opportunities, and threats of your church. Use four tear sheets to record the results of this brainstorming session. Every church can benefit from looking at its strengths, but you will find that many of your plans emerge from the list of your weaknesses and opportunities. Strengths are often already addressed in your church's activities, but weaknesses and opportunities cry out for action.

Planning According to the Five Functions

Teach your people about the five functions.—Evangelism is reaching people for Christ. Discipleship takes place any time one believer engages another, and both become more like Christ. Fellowship is more than cookies and ice cream in the fellowship hall; it is also believers coming together to help one another shoulder the burdens they carry. Ministry is believers meeting needs in Jesus name. Worship is an encounter with God.

Consider each of the functions one at a time.—What has the church done in the past in evangelism? Evaluate the effectiveness of past actions: Choose the highest priorities and plan to carry them out. By intentionally reviewing, considering possibilities, and choosing actions related to each of the five functions, the church will achieve both balance and focus.

A church that practices each of these five functions in a healthy manner can expect to grow. But church growth is not the goal of the church. Church growth is the result of a church's doing the five things every church ought to do.

Resources

Mims, Gene. *Kingdom Principles for Church Growth,* revised and expanded. Nashville: LifeWay Press, 2001.
Warren, Rick. *The Purpose Driven Church*. Grand Rapids: Zondervan Publishing House, 1995.

5. (HOW TO) Develop Purpose and Vision Statements for Your Church

Why does your church exist? The answer may seem so obvious that it needs no answer, but the question deserves your attention.

In *The Purpose Driven Church* Rick Warren rightly pointed out that every church is driven by something.

Some churches are driven by money.—In those churches, the main question is, How much is this going to cost?

Some churches are driven by buildings.—In those churches, the building dictates the programs or ministries. These churches may ignore ministries they have the facilities to carry out because they don't want their precious buildings to be disturbed.

Some churches are driven by tradition.—They are often heard to say, "We've never done it that way before."

Some churches are driven by personality.—Sorry, Pastor, but it's probably not driven by your personality. The driving personality is that person who can determine the outcome of a vote at business meeting. He or she may even be able to do that without even saying a word or by making a few phone calls and exerting tremendous influence.

According to Warren, every church ought to be driven by its purpose. There is tremendous benefit in a church determining its purpose.

A purpose statement is a restatement of the Great Commission in contemporary terms. For example, "Our church will fulfill our Lord's command to reach, baptize, and teach those in our community by the power and presence of the Holy Spirit." The statement needs to be concise and well written in order to communicate with the body of believers.

A vision statement is a compelling declaration that clarifies how the church intends to fulfill the Great Commission in its setting. For example, "Our church will fulfill the Great Commission by sharing the love of God in Christ with every person through evangelism, discipleship, ministry, fellowship, and worship." The vision statement should be clear, well written, easy to remember, and easy to communicate.

One word of caution: Some churches can get bogged down in their effort to develop these statements. In fact, some churches have been known to spend up to a year in the effort. Set a completion date at the beginning of this process. Suggest to the team that three months is sufficient time to complete the statements. Lead the team to commit themselves to finish this important work by that completion date. If that date draws near and the work is not complete, ask the team to spend an entire day and finish the work before they leave on that day. You may be surprised at how much can be accomplished during one day.

Some people live and work in a business environment that speaks the language of purpose and vision statements. These leaders will understand the importance of developing such statements. Others may need strong but loving pastoral leadership to help them see the value.

Some people, especially in rural communities or older churches, may never see the need of purpose and vision statements. They have a different mind-set. They don't speak the language of "core values" or "vision statements." Some might even ask, "Preacher, don't you know what our purpose is?"

Some churches will not invest three months to develop a purpose statement, but they would enjoy spending a Sunday night service discussing why God planted a church in their community. The result of this Sunday night conversation might be thought of as a consensus purpose statement. It should help your people view their ministries and actions through the important lens of purpose.

Resource

Warren, Rick. *The Purpose Driven Church*. Grand Rapids: Zondervan
    Publishing House, 1995.

6. (HOW TO) Avoid the Trap of Sexual Misconduct

Only a few things can destroy your ministry as a pastor. Sexual misconduct is definitely one of those things. What begins as a friendship or counseling relationship can become a sinful affair. Even if the relationship never actually becomes adulterous, an inappropriate sexual relationship can destroy your ministry, hurt your family, and damage your church. Here are a few tips to help you avoid the trap of sexual misconduct.

Don't put yourself in a dangerous situation.—The attention of an attractive woman may be flattering, but even the best of people can do the worst of things.

Minimize the risk.—Never counsel a woman alone. Try to have your secretary, or someone, in the outer office or an adjacent room when counseling. Perhaps you could ask a senior adult woman to answer the phone while you counsel.

Know when to refer.—Limit your counseling sessions to one or two, for no longer than one hour in duration. If a woman needs more counseling than this, you probably should refer her to a professional. You are not a professional counselor. Do not represent or refer to yourself as a professional counselor.

Keep your own marriage healthy.—Life in the parsonage may be stressful, but your home can be happy and healthy.

Do not touch the women you counsel.—A person in need of counseling may be vulnerable enough to misinterpret even an innocent hug. Don't even hold hands while you pray.

Keep your spiritual life strong.—Spend time with God every day. Watch out for the following warning signs.
- You find yourself looking forward to someone's visits, thinking: *What shall I wear today? Will she like this?*
- You rearrange your schedule to accommodate time spent with a

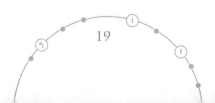

woman, even "legitimate church business."
- You meet in inappropriate locations—at lunch, in her home, in your office after hours.
- You find yourself nurturing fantasy. When pastors fall, that fall is never sudden. Only the discovery of the fall is sudden. The fall is the result of wrong thinking that began well in advance of the affair.
- You begin to withhold information about your activities from your spouse.

A survey by *Leadership* magazine revealed that almost one clergyman in four admits to engaging in inappropriate sexual conduct.[1] Some pastors think they are safe because they do not perceive themselves to be "handsome" or "attractive." Remember, people are attracted to others for many different reasons, including power, influence, and prestige. Pastors must constantly be on guard against this temptation.

Giving in to sexual temptation can cost you and your church dearly. Your family will be hurt. Your church can be sued. Your reputation will be destroyed. Your ministry will be finished. The other person and her family will be deeply hurt. Ask any pastor who has fallen. It's a trick from Satan. It's not worth it.

These are strong reasons for avoiding sexual misconduct. But there is a more powerful reason. Sexual misconduct is sin. Your ethical, moral actions will please Jesus, the One before whom you will one day stand to give account.

Adapted from Paul Powell, *Shepherding the Sheep in Smaller Churches* (Dallas: Annuity Board of the Southern Baptist Convention, 1995), 92.

---

[1]Bob Moeller, "The Sex Life of America's Christians," *Leadership*, Summer 1995, XVI:30-31.

Resource
Reccord, Bob. *Beneath the Surface*. Nashville: Broadman & Holman, 2002.

7. (HOW TO) Get Along with Church Members

How to get along with people cannot be fully learned from a textbook or in the seminary classroom. These skills must be hammered out on the anvil of experience. Here are a few basic principles to help any pastor with those all-important people skills.

Love and Trust People

Love and trust must be intentionally cultivated. Commit yourself as a pastor to approach your people, even the difficult ones, in this manner. Even though your attitude of love and trust may not always be returned in kind, your risk will be worthwhile. But how do you love the unlovely and trust those who are not always trustworthy?

Develop a healthy appreciation for others.—Perceive them as persons of worth. An attitude of suspicion is the only alternative, and suspicion is a waste.

Develop a healthy concept of God.—This will give you a proper perspective on your concept of self and others. If you, as a pastor, view God as primarily a God of wrath and judgment, this will be reflected in your concept of God. If the pastor recognizes God's attributes of love and forgiveness, the pastor's own love and forgiveness will be more apparent.

Develop a healthy concept of authority. It is much easier for a pastor to love and trust if he isn't obsessed with a need to control and manipulate.

Practice Honesty and Openness

An honest pastor is a man of integrity. The word *integrity* comes from the mathematical term *integer,* which means "whole or undivided." An honest pastor does not have many sides; he is a man of integrity.

Openness takes the pastor one step beyond honesty. Openness implies vulnerability.

Honesty and openness may sometimes carry risk in the church. The open, honest pastor may encounter people in his church who are disappointed when their pastor shows his humanity. These persons may be devoted to the pastor and love him until he shows his human side. Nevertheless, vulnerability is worth the effort for pastors who want to relate to members as team members.

Realize the Futility of Withdrawal and Avoidance

A pastor can learn to love and trust if he realizes the futility of withdrawal and avoidance. Some pastors practice this by moving to another church every time a difficulty arises. Others simply withdraw emotionally with almost the same result.

Here are some negative and positive suggestions for improving relationships with church members.

Things to Avoid

• Avoid being judgmental.
• Avoid hypercriticism.
• Avoid unrealistic expectations.
• Avoid ambiguity or inconsistency.

Steps to Take

• Cultivate a genuine desire to help people.
• Develop a willingness to forgive people.
• Adopt an attitude of forgiveness toward people.
• Learn to trust people.
• Develop sensitivity toward people.
• Maintain flexibility in dealing with people.
• Deal with frustrations that come from relating to people.
• Acknowledge your personal limitations in dealing with people.
• Seek opportunities to develop close relationships with people.

Give some quality attention to getting along with people in your church. Through exhibiting love, trust, honesty, and openness, the pastor can create an environment in his church where close interpersonal relationships can develop.

Adapted from Brooks Faulkner, *Getting on Top of Your Work* , *A Manual for the 21st-Century Minister,* (Nashville: Convention Press, 1999).

8. (HOW TO) Delegate: Giving Your Job Away

Some church members expect their pastors to be supermen. They must be preacher, leader, business manager, caring pastor, active community member, and more. Of course, the standard is often impossibly high. The wise pastor can multiply his ministry by involving others in working toward the mission of the church.

Delegating to Paid Staff Members

In many churches the pastor leads a staff team. It is reasonable that he should delegate to the church staff.

Before delegation occurs, the pastor and staff members must have covenanted together to (1) do the work of the church, (2) be committed to one another in a relationship of trust, and (3) be committed to personal growth in the love of Christ.

Delegating to staff members should be based on job descriptions that give staff members a sense of confidence in areas of responsibility. Since the pastor is the leader of the church, the job descriptions should be developed with the pastor as supervisor. Larger staffs may be organized with different levels of staff supervision, but the pastor is the leader of the church staff.

Reporting and evaluation must also be practiced if delegating is to be effective. Weekly staff meeting, or team meeting, is a good time for reporting and evaluation.

Some pastors find delegation difficult. Delegation is a skill that must be learned and practiced. Here are a few attitudes to be overcome.

Inability to let go.—In a small but growing church the pastor has always led the Sunday School. As the church grows and the need for a minister of education becomes apparent, the pastor may resist letting someone else lead the Sunday School.

Lack of confidence.—If the pastor doubts the competency of the staff, he may find it easier to do the task himself. It would be better for the pastor to equip and train the staff member.

23

Fear of competition.—Most pastors have inside them a desire to achieve. Some pastors don't delegate because they want to look good in comparison to the staff.

Lack of time.—It's ironic, but true. Some pastors decide, *It would be quicker to do this myself than to teach someone else to do it.* Yes, growing people takes time, but it is a worthwhile investment.

Tips for Successful Delegating to Staff Members or Volunteers

Secure mutual agreement.—Determine the task to be done and how accountability will be carried out.

Seek the right person.—An effective delegator will match people with tasks. Consider the skills and abilities of the person, but don't forget to pray.

Seek to motivate.—Use encouragement freely. Publicly acknowledge those who are doing a good job.

Develop understanding.—Make sure what is delegated is fully understood. Give clear, simple instructions.

Allow for mistakes.—The person who makes no mistakes is not attempting anything challenging or worthwhile. Hold volunteers and staff members accountable, but allow for inevitable mistakes.

Encourage initiative.—Growing, gifted, skilled people will enjoy taking some initiative in new actions. Encourage this in those to whom you delegate.

Be persistent.—Don't give up on the person to whom authority is delegated. Bless them with enough time to find their way and succeed.

Expect results.—No need to apologize. If you have enough confidence in people to delegate a task to them, let them know that you expect them to succeed.

Adapted from Brooks Faulkner, *Getting on Top of Your Work* , *A Manual for the 21st-Century Minister,* (Nashville: Convention Press, 1999).

9. (HOW TO) Deal with a Pastor Search Committee

Most pastors and their families can spot them a mile away–the pastor search committee. Many times they just show up in time for the morning worship. Even when they split up and sit in two groups, they stick out like a sore thumb. The pastor begins to preach, knowing that every word is being analyzed.

The coming of a pastor search committee stirs lots of feelings in the hearts of the pastor and his family. There is a sense of excitement. He wonders where they are from and what the church is like. There is also a sense of dread. If this move really happens, the pastor will leave people he loves, uproot his family, and begin a new chapter of his life.

Here are a few tips for dealing with the pastor search committee appropriately and effectively.

Don't feel or act as though you are on trial.–Approach this process with confidence. You seek only the will of God. You are not an applicant to be pastor of their church. If God does not lead you to go to this new church, He will provide for you in the place where you are serving.

Be yourself.–You have nothing to prove. It's appropriate to make the best impression you can, but don't pretend to be something you are not.

Let God control the process.–Don't push or politic for this new church to call you. Changing churches will not solve all your problems.

Talk with a trusted friend about why you want (or don't want) to make this move.–Get in touch with your feelings and their source. All ministers go through hardships. Running from your problems is usually a mistake. The best solution may be to stay, see the problems through, and then move with confidence that your motives are right.

Ask the committee for information about the prospective church.–If the committee is well trained, they will offer you a packet of information about their church and community. If they don't offer it, request it. This will help you pray intelligently.

If possible, drive through the community where the prospective church is located.

If the committee's talks with you become serious, consider scheduling more than one meeting with them.

Ask the committee for an honest appraisal of the church.—Explain that you have been open about yourself and that you would like the committee to be just as open about the church they represent.

If the talks continue to the point of scheduling a visit to the church "in view of a call, discuss expectations and the terms of the call.—As you seek to do the will of God, remember that these terms may not dictate whether you accept the call, but a considerate committee will want to settle these questions before the prospective pastor is presented to the church. Here are a few items to consider:

• Salary	• Role of the wife
• Moving expenses	• Church growth patterns
• Auto expenses	• Doctrinal beliefs
• Housing	• Tenure of past pastors
• Benefits	• Leadership style
• Vacation and days off	• Community involvement
• Time away for revivals and conferences	• Deacon ministry (board or servant)
• Pulpit supply	• Denominational involvement

Ask the pastor search committee to dream.—Invite them to describe their church in 1 year, 5 years, and 10 years. You can learn a lot about the church as you listen to these key and trusted leaders dream about the future.

Adapted from Gary Hardin, "Being Intentional with a Search Committee," *Church Administration* (March 1991), 3.

Resource
Pastor Search Committee Handbook. Nashville: LifeWay Press, 2002.

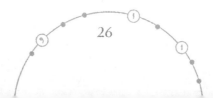

10. (HOW TO) Dedicate a Building

Few things a church can do require more energy and resources than
building a building. When the building is finished, people usually feel a
sense of pride and accomplishment. They have invested much of their time,
energy, and dollars in the project.

Considering the Value of a Building Dedication

*A building dedication gives the church an opportunity to celebrate a significant
accomplishment.*—Whether the facility is large or small, extravagant or practical, the church probably has reason to celebrate. This in not inappropriate
pride. The church will and should give God the glory, but recognizing the
completion of a building as an important accomplishment is right and good.

*A building dedication gives the church an opportunity to thank God and
give Him glory.*—The service of dedication is a spiritual service. It is also a
public service. The dedication may be attended by many members and
neighbors. Give God the glory for all that has been accomplished to make
the dream of a building a reality.

*A building dedication is an opportunity for the church to look to the
future.*—The pastor and people have many wonderful dreams about how
the building will be used in the service of God. Share those dreams. Set the
stage for future ministries, and activities. Invite the church to participate in
using the facility to its maximum advantage.

*A building dedication is an opportunity to interpret the focus of your church
to the community.*—Local officials, contractors, and neighbors will probably
attend the dedication. They certainly should be invited. Many of them have
no idea, or a very mistaken idea, about your church. Use the dedication
service to interpret the work of your church to them.

Planning the Day's Events

One key to a successful dedication is good planning. The pastor should
probably take the lead, but a resource group including key leaders in the

church and some of those active in the building project might help. Be sure to consider the following.
- Involvement of community leaders.
- Participation by denominational representatives.
- Former pastors, staff members, and church members.
- A professional photographer.
- Invitation to local newspaper or other media.
- Recognition of members who have served well during the project.
- A well-planned, printed worship program.
- A display or printed piece that tells some history of the church and this project.
- An afternoon meal.
- A tour of the new facility.

Developing a Dedication Service

Plan a service as the Lord leads. It should match your church, your needs, and your facility. Maybe this sample service will help you get started.

An Order of Worship for Building Dedication Day

Call to Worship	Psalm 103:1-5
Invocation	
Hymn	"To God Be the Glory"
Responsive Reading	
Introduction of Special Guests	
Greetings from Civic/Denominational Representatives	
Offertory Hymn	
Worship with Tithes and Offerings	
Gospel in Song (choir or other)	
Sermon	Pastor
Hymn of Commitment	"Jesus Is Lord of All"
Benediction	

---

11. **HOW TO** Ordain a Minister

Ordination is setting apart one who has responded to God's call to the gospel ministry. Although exact steps and procedures vary according to local custom, here are some basics.

- A candidate for the ministry is usually licensed by his church soon after he indicates that God has called him into the ministry. The licensing is the church's tentative approval for a man to serve until he has proved himself qualified for ordination.
- Ordination usually takes place when a minister begins serving in a church. The ordination may be at the candidate's church of service or home church.
- The church will set an appropriate date and authorize forming an ordination council to examine the candidate as to his fitness for ordination. This council is usually made up of ministers and deacons.
- The candidate should be examined concerning his conversion, call to ministry, doctrinal views, leadership style, commitment, character, and daily walk with the Lord.
- When the examination is completed, the ordination council should present a recommendation that the church proceed with the ordination of the candidate. The council may choose to delay the ordination or even reject the candidate. That is why it may be best to hold the council one week prior to the ordination service.

Sample Ordination Service

Call to Worship

Hymn of Praise

Scripture and Prayer

Introductory Statement

    (Tell why you have gathered.)

Presentation of the Candidate and His Family

The Ordination Prayer

    (Candidate will kneel facing the congregation.)

Laying on of Hands

(While the candidate is kneeling, ordained men in the
congregation will file by and place their hands on the
candidate's head and whisper a prayer, encouraging
word, or admonition to the candidate.)

Presentation of the Bible

Special Music

Message

Hymn of Commitment

(Remember, God may choose this time to call someone
else into the ministry.)

The entire congregation will greet the candidate and his family.

The church should not be hasty in ordaining an individual. It should be certain he has the scriptural qualifications to serve as a minister. The candidate should prove himself before he is considered for ordination.

Once a man has been ordained, he should live an exemplary Christian life and show himself to be a maturing, growing leader in the service of Christ. He is responsible to Jesus, his Lord, and to the church to behave as a God-called minister of the gospel.

Adapted from *MBC Pastor's Manual*, prepared by the Small Church Network, Missouri Baptist Convention.

12. (HOW TO) Deal with Ineffective Workers

A preschool worker loves children and is faithful in attendance. But every Sunday he is late. Parents and other workers are frustrated and inconvenienced.

A teacher of teenage girls is always unprepared to teach. She is well liked by the teens, but most Sunday School time is spent discussing schoolwork or TV. Rarely do they get around to Bible study.

One of the most difficult problems faced by pastors today is how to deal with ineffective workers. Here are a few ideas.

Understand Why Workers Are Ineffective
• Workers may be serving with the wrong age group.
• Workers may be serving in wrong kinds of positions.
• Workers may not understand what they are supposed to do.
• Workers may be experiencing health or personal problems.
• Workers may not have been enlisted properly.
• Workers may have too many jobs in the church.

Deal with Ineffective Workers Positively
• Talk with the person face-to-face.
• Pray with the person.
• Provide some options. In what other positions might this person serve?
• Enlist people properly.
• Encourage attendance at team meetings.
• Compliment them on something they are doing well.
• Provide all workers a list of training opportunities and encourage participation.
• Show continuing concern for all workers.

Consider These Guidelines

Don't prolong the situation.—You may choose to delay action because the ineffective worker is in training or because prayerful deliberation suggests that the time for action has not yet come, but do not put off the action you know you should take now.

When in doubt, consider the group involved.—An ineffective worker in the preschool department may demand more immediate attention than an ineffective worker in an adult men's class. Both are important, but adults may be better able to care for themselves. Both situations need your attention and action, but consider the group.

Consider giving the ineffective worker a leave of absence.—Most ineffective workers realize they are ineffective and that something must be done. A leave of absence may be welcomed (and it may not).

Provide resources workers need to be the best they can be.—Make sure they have the best teaching materials or other resources. Also provide training resources.

Continue to help ineffective workers and be patient as long as they recognize a need to change and are willing to improve.—You are a pastor. These ineffective workers are members of your team. Don't be hasty in removing them from the positions in which they were enlisted to serve.

Only when all else has failed and the worker feels no need for improvement should he or she be relieved of his or her responsibility.—Take this action with love and yet firmness. Striving for excellence in the ministries of your church is important, but remember that you are dealing with a person.

Remember, the worker probably knows he or she is ineffective but feels he or she made a commitment and must abide by that.—Work with the person to come up with a win-win solution.

Adapted from *Great Commission Breakthrough : "How to" Ideas for Great Commission Churches* (Nashville: Sunday School Division Office, The Sunday School Board of the Southern Baptist Convention, 1992), 5.

13. (HOW TO) Deal with Criticism

Some criticism is frivolous. Someone doesn't like your clothes or hair.

Some criticism is personal. Your family isn't the perfect model they expected.

Some criticism is serious. Your preaching isn't what it should be.

Almost all criticism is painful.

We cannot control whether we will face criticism. It will come. We cannot always control when criticism comes, but we can control our reaction to it.

Realize that criticism will certainly come.—The "honeymoon" is that period of time when you have recently come to be pastor of a church and you can seemingly do no wrong. All your ideas are fresh and new. The people have not yet seen you fail. Your few mistakes are overlooked because you are new (you just didn't know any better). But the time comes when the honeymoon is over. Reality sets in for the pastor and the people. Be ready, criticism will come.

Make a distinction between the person and the criticism.—Remember that the person who is making critical statements is not the enemy. Your criticism may come from one who is a spiritual baby. He or she may be backslidden. Your critic may be misguided by some manipulative other person. Or the criticism may even be right and justified. In any case, the critic is not the enemy. Very likely, your critic loves God and wants what is best for the church.

Continue to love those who criticize you.—Continue to be their pastor. Minister to them at every opportunity. Ask yourself what Jesus would do in this situation and do your best to be like Him. Many times in my ministry I have continued to love, and even serve, critical persons, while they criticized me. Sometimes, not always, these critical persons have become some of my best friends and strongest supporters. How you react to criticism is a demonstration of your maturity and confidence. Don't become defensive. Resist the temptation to strike back. It is unflattering and counterproductive.

Honestly attempt to determine whether the criticism might be valid.–Even if the criticism is not deserved, you may be able to learn from it. Remember the principle of Romans 8:28. Since we know that "all things work together for good," God may intend for something good to come from this criticism.

Ask yourself these questions: Is the criticism meant to be constructive or destructive? Can I improve myself or my ministry by accepting this criticism as constructive? Is pride keeping me from hearing an important message?

Consider the source of the criticism.–Why is this person expressing criticism? Is there a pattern of a critical spirit in this person? Is the critic usually negative? Is this person motivated by factors other than the obvious?

Don't allow unjustified or destructive criticism to get you off track.– Criticism can be discouraging. A discouraged pastor is often an inactive pastor. When you are immobilized by discouragement, you are less effective for the Lord; and you are most vulnerable to your enemies. If you humbly and honestly search your heart and believe the criticism to be unjustified, continue to serve God and lead the church. Continue to love and serve your people, even the critical ones. Demonstrate patience and perseverance. Don't let discouragement immobilize you.

Apologize when appropriate.–If you have miscommunicated or behaved in an inappropriate way or harbored an inappropriate attitude, be mature enough to apologize. Your stature as a leader will increase in the eyes of your people.

Adapted from Willie Beaty, "How to Deal with Criticism," *Great Commission Breakthrough: "How to" Ideas for Great Commission Churches* (Nashville: Sunday School Division Office, The Sunday School Board of the Southern Baptist Convention, 1992), 30.

14. (HOW TO) Know When It Is Time to Leave

The decision to leave a church is often filled with emotion. Here are some suggestions that may bring some clarity to the issue.

Calling
Ideally, leaving is a matter of God's calling. Even if the church is growing and ministry is meaningful, when God pulls at you to leave, pay attention. If that pull is strong, clear, and persistent, it may well be the Lord's signal that it is time to leave. Seek counsel from a trusted friend before deciding. A multitude of counselors offers safety (see Prov. 24:6).

Circumstances
Circumstances sometimes make it necessary to leave. For example, family health problems, special education needs for children, financial necessities, persecution, and safety for your family.

Competencies
If the church has outgrown your ability to serve effectively, and you see no opportunity for your skills to grow and develop further, and you become a hindrance to the future growth and ministry of the church, it may be time to step aside. On the other hand, you may have outgrown the church. If you stay, you will stagnate. Leaving, therefore, is not arrogance but simply good stewardship of God's resources manifested in you.

Depletion
Anyone can burn out. When your energy, focus, enthusiasm, and joy are emptied out, a decision is needed. Be careful that the decision to leave is not made in haste when burnout is involved. Perhaps a leave of absence for recovery and renewal is a possibility. If so, take it. If the church is impatient with your renewal time and you can't give any more energy to the ministry there, consider starting the process for leaving.

Conflict
All churches have conflict. However, when conflict over your ministry and leadership is dividing, damaging, and destroying the fellowship and mission

of the church, leaving is an option. Some churches are pathologically dysfunctional and can damage you and your family. You become the scapegoat for their anger and frustration. Leaving can be justified. Don't remain until you or your family are seriously hurt.

Tenure

Sometimes the length of a pastor's stay can reach a point of diminishing return. When you and the church are slipping in vision, enthusiasm, and zeal, and staying is creating a negative backlash, then relocation may be the best thing for you and the church.

Conduct

When unethical conduct such as lying, cheating, sexual misconduct, or stealing has destroyed the people's trust and support, the wise decision is to leave.

Doctrine

Doctrinal unity is essential for a healthy church. If your theological and doctrinal beliefs are fundamentally counter to that of the church to the degree that it threatens the fellowship of the church, then integrity may call for you to leave.

Livelihood

Ministers must make a living to minister. If the church cannot provide a livelihood, then you must either leave or enter bivocational ministry. Caring for your family is a high and biblical priority. Thousands of wonderful ministers are bivocational. Don't hesitate to consider this honorable way of doing ministry.

In the final analysis, no one of these factors, taken alone, should cause you to leave a place where God has called you to serve. The Holy Spirit of God may overrule every suggestion in this article and instruct you to stay just where you are. Do your best to determine prayerfully the will of God, and follow His plan. These suggestions may help you determine what He wants you to do.

Adapted from Norris Smith, "When Is It Time to Leave?" *MBC Pastor's Manual* (Small Church Network, Missouri Baptist Convention), D25–26.

15. (HOW TO) Constitute a New Church

To be present at the formal constitution of a new church is exciting and awe inspiring. The constitution service is the culmination of significant events which have gone before.

Some churches are begun as missions of another congregation. These new churches have a spiritual family who have been supportive and helpful along the way. Someone or some group likely prayed and longed for the day when a healthy church would be established in that place. The constitution service will be planned with appropriate honor for those who have dreamed, prayed, and worked for this day.

Some churches are begun after some person or small group of persons starts a Bible study or worship service in a community. A church may be born without the help of a sponsoring church. The constitution service in a church like this should honor those who invested themselves in the new church.

Some churches come into existence because of a split in another congregation. Many of these churches overcome their sad beginning and mature into healthy, effective congregations. In these situations the constitution service should focus on the future of the new church. Remember that many of the people involved in the new church are wounded and hurting.

Regardless of the reason for the existence of the new church, the constitution service should be approached with a sense of dignity. Yet it should be a celebration, never dry and boring, but reflective of the joy and anticipation in the hearts of the people in the new church. Here are some things to consider as you approach constituting a church.

- Set a date to constitute.
- Seek assistance and information from denominational leaders such as the associational director of missions.
- Invite neighboring churches of like faith and order to send representatives to form a council.
- If the new church is a mission of an existing church, the sponsoring church should be vitally involved in the process.
- This council will meet prior to the constituting service to choose a moderator or clerk and constitute the church.

A Service of Constitution

Devotional
Song   "The Church's One Foundation"
Scripture Reading   Matthew 16:18-19;
                              Acts 2:41-42;
                              I Corinthians 12:27;
                              Ephesians 4:11-13;
                              Colossians 1:18
Prayer
A Look at the Church's History
Welcome and Recognition of Guests
Statement of Purpose of This Meeting
Recommendation of the Sponsoring Church
    (This is read by the sponsoring church and approved by
the constituting church.)
Roll Call of Members' Names
Election of Officers and Committees of the New Church
    (The moderator of the council may serve as temporary
moderator for further proceedings. The names of church
officers and committees are presented for election. A pastor
should be called according to the plan previously adopted.)

Worship Service

Hymn   "To God Be the Glory"
Offering
Sermon
    (Should include a charge to the pastor and people.)
Invitation for New Members
Reception of New Members
Benediction

16. (HOW TO) Call Out the Called in Your Church

Pastors have the blessed privilege of creating an atmosphere where young people and others can hear and respond to God's call upon their lives. It is vitally important that pastors create that atmosphere for all people as God calls them into service for Him. It is also vital that pastors create that atmosphere where people can respond to God's call to ministry. While God calls every believer to serve Him, God calls some to be pastors, evangelists, ministers, and teachers of all kinds. This special calling into vocational or bivocational ministry is what Neil Knierim called "the cornerstone for effective ministry."

Here are some ideas to help you intentionally call out the called in your congregation.

Preach the Word of God Boldly

In your preaching, emphasize how God uses men and women to accomplish His purpose on earth. Tell stories of those biblical heroes of the faith. Preach a message designed especially to challenge young people and others to hear the voice of God and offer themselves at his altar.

Expose Young People and Others to Those Who Have Made a Difference

Bring to your pulpit men and women who have been used of God in a powerful way in His kingdom. Missionaries, pastors, evangelists, and other ministers can be a powerful role model for those with whom God may be dealing. Try to make it possible for those who have acknowledged God's call or may be dealing with that issue to spend time with the hero. Take these same groups to conventions and meetings where they will hear and meet people who are used powerfully of God.

Pray for a Spirit of Revival

The revival meeting held once or twice a year is important. God may choose these times to make His call clear to someone in your church. But a spirit of revival should be present the rest of the year. Provide time for testimonies throughout the year. When someone is called to preach, let him exercise his gift in your pulpit.

Depend Completely on the Holy Spirit
Ask God to fill you and your people with His Spirit to create a sense of openness as the Lord speaks to individuals about His will for their lives.

Provide Witnessing and Soul-winning Opportunities
Provide witness training and opportunities to all the congregation. Personally invite those who have been or may be called to the ministry. Also provide opportunities for missions work to these same people. Mission trips are precious times when young people and others can exercise their gifts.

Lift up the example of those who have gone out from your church to serve the Lord. Pray for them. Recognize them when they return home for a visit. Celebrate the victories God brings to their ministries.

Calling out the called is a great joy for any pastor. Whether you are privileged to pastor one who is called or a hundred, lift up and celebrate God's calling and sending out people to serve Him vocationally or bivocationally.

Adapted from Richard P. Oldham, "Building a Climate for Calling Out the Called," *Church Administration*, April 98, 3–7.

Resource
Knierim Neil and Yvonne Burrage. *God's Call: The Cornerstone of Effective Ministry.* Nashville: Convention Press, 1997.

17. (HOW TO) Prepare a Sermon

The Bible is the Word of God. It is "truth without any mixture of error."[1]
The Bible is truth. It is relevant to people today, and contemporary people
who will hear your message need to encounter that truth.

I am convinced that expository preaching is the best kind of preaching.
In *Surviving and Thriving in Today's Ministry,* Don Mathis gave some strong
benefits to expository preaching.

- Expository preaching is a style that corresponds to the biblical pattern
  of preaching and to the way the Bible was written.
- Expository preaching meets every conceivable spiritual need and makes
  for a well-instructed people.
- Expository preaching prevents the pastor from wasting valuable time
  searching for a text or topic for his sermon.
- Expository preaching insists that the preacher study and prepare well.
  Preaching expository sermons that meet needs and present the
  relevancy of Scripture in a way people can understand it is not easy.
- Expository preaching forces the preacher to preach passages and to
  address needs that neither you nor the congregation would choose.
  It will lead you to preach the whole Bible.
- When you address a sensitive subject, people will not be inclined to
  think you are preaching to or about a particular situation.

Many books have been written on the subject of how to prepare a
sermon. This small article is in no way suggested as an adequate substitute
for studying those wonderful works on preaching.

Here are some simple basics to developing the sermon that has served
many preachers well.

Start with the Bible.—This may seem so obvious it doesn't need
mentioning. But the reality is, some preachers start with a subject, then
find supporting verses. This is not to say a preacher should never preach
a topical sermon. I believe, however, that exposition should be the norm.

Discover the central truth of the passage.—What truth is God presenting
to His people? Pray that God will reveal His truth to you. Ask God to lead
you to the truth He wants you to develop for this message.

Do a thorough study of the biblical text.—Dig into the passage and learn

all you can about it.

Study the original languages.–If you have no formal training in Greek and Hebrew, you can accomplish much with a *Strong's Concordance*.

Study the historical context.–Learn about the biblical writer. Discover all you can about the people to whom the Holy Spirit spoke through him.

Study related passages.–What else does the Bible have to say about this truth or theme. What else did God say to these people?

Develop a concise statement of the central truth.–Boil it down. Your emerging sermon should have a simple, easy-to-remember theme. Keep working on it until it is logical and clear.

Now go back and develop supporting ideas from the text.–For example, the central truth of Mark 2:1-9 is that every person needs an encounter with Jesus. Supporting ideas include:
- Bringing people to Jesus is hard work.
- Bringing people to Jesus is a real effort.
- Bringing people to Jesus will always meet opposition.
- Bringing people to Jesus requires a creative approach.
- Bringing people to Jesus results in changed lives.

Nail down the application.–Preaching is not just teaching Bible history. It is presenting a relevant truth from God's Word in a way people can understand and apply it. Pray that God will show you how this truth is relevant.

Determine the best way to communicate this truth to God's people.–Make sure the entire outline is logical and clear. Develop illustrations that reveal the central truth.

---

[1]Herschel H. Hobbs, *The Baptist Faith and Message: Revised Edition* (Nashville: Convention Press, 1996).
[2]Don R. Mathis, *Surviving and Thriving in Today's Ministry: Prescription for Effective Leadership* (Nashville: Convention Press, 1997), 41-.50

18. **HOW TO** Preach Through a Book of the Bible

For several years now, I have ministered through LifeWay Christian Resources. Even though I preach almost every Sunday, I still miss some parts of pastoring. I miss preaching to the same people week after week, and I miss preaching through books of the Bible. If you have never experienced preaching through a book of the Bible, prayerfully consider doing so. It is very rewarding.

Benefits of Preaching Through Books of the Bible

It helps the preacher to have a disciplined approach to studying and preaching.—There are many demands on the time of the pastor. He could fill every day with good activities and leave little or no time for study. When the entire congregation knows you will preach from a certain book the following Sunday night or Wednesday night, you will be encouraged to give study from that book a higher priority.

It produces a well-fed congregation.—Preaching through books of the Bible has provided a balance to the spiritual diet received through my preaching. The Bible is a balanced and perfect book. When we faithfully preach it, people will not lack.

It helps us avoid preaching only (or almost only) on our pet subjects.

You know what you will be preaching next week.—Throughout the week, you can watch for appropriate illustrations. God can begin weeks in advance to open the truth of His passage for a certain sermon.

Your preaching reflects how the Bible was written.—I have complete confidence in the Bible. It is reasonable to preach the Word of God just as it was written. This approach allows the congregation to become familiar with an entire book of the Bible.

It forces the preacher to do a serious study of the text.—Dealing with an

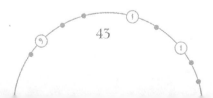

entire book of the Bible in a shallow manner will be painfully obvious to all who hear.

A Simple Process for Preaching Through a Book of the Bible

Read the book of the Bible.—Imagine that you are one of the Old or New Testament people to whom the book was originally addressed. Study will come next; for now just read the entire book.

Study the book.—Do a thorough exegesis. Find some helpful study aids and use them. (You can build your library by purchasing a few books on each book of the Bible as you preach them. As the years roll by, you will develop an excellent research library.) Discover the historical context in which the book was written. Learn all you can about the author.

Outline the themes or truths in the book.—Even though you will find many outlines available in the body of study materials, develop your own outline. Prayerfully search for God's message revealed in that book.

Nail down the main themes of each message to be preached.—This is the hard work of sermon preparation. Pray. Study. Ask God about the sermons you will preach. Sometimes several messages will come from a single verse. Other times, a message will be found in a longer passage, perhaps several chapters.

Decide when the sermons will be preached.—Sunday nights or Wednesday nights are good times for preaching through books of the Bible. If you choose to preach through a book of the Bible on Sunday mornings, consider the number of times the series will be interrupted for seasonal sermons.

Preach the Word.—With the confidence that comes from knowing you are preaching all the Word in a disciplined manner, deliver the messages God lays on your heart.

Resource
Harold Bryson. *Expository Preaching*. Nashville: Broadman & Holman, 1995.

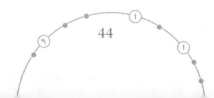

19. (HOW TO) File Sermon Illustrations

This is a simple process for filing sermon illustrations. In fact, it may be too simple for some. I have never found time or inclination to put sermon illustrations in my computer. I have never been comfortable with a complicated system of numbers and cross-references. I need a simple, quick system that will provide a place to put sermon illustrations and will allow me to find them again when I need them. Here's what works for me.

Start with 12 File Folders

Label one for each month of the year. Place these folders in a convenient place. For me this is the file drawer in my desk. About half of the sermon illustrations I find can be filed in one of these 12 folders. If, for example, I am visiting the hospital and see a real-life illustration of a mother's love as she cares for a sick child, I make a note about the illustration. That note goes in the folder labeled *May*. Mother's Day is in May, and I can thumb through all the items in that folder and find lots of illustrations on the family or motherhood. If I am skimming a magazine and find a good illustration on Christmas, I know where to put it. Christmas illustrations go in the folder labeled *December*. Illustrations related to thankfulness go in the *November* folder, etc.

Add Folders with Subject Headings Behind the 12 Monthly Folders

Not every illustration fits in the 12 monthly folders. Add file folders with appropriate subject headings, and place them behind the 12. Add as many of these as needed. When I find an illustration about how angels protect people at God's command, I label a folder with the word
and place the illustration in the folder.

One might ask, "Why not place all illustrations in folders according to subject?" For me, the folders became too numerous to use effectively. About half the illustrations will be filed according to the month I expect to use them.

Develop the Habit of Constantly Searching for Illustrations

I own a couple of those books of illustrations. I almost never use them.

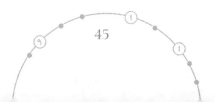

I have found that the best illustrations come from my life and experience. When an illustration has the benefit of firsthand experience, it has credibility. Carry note cards in your pocket. Make notes as soon as possible after seeing or experiencing an illustration. File it right away.

Be Sure to Credit the Source of the Illustration
Keep a record of the source with the illustration. Integrity demands that we tell the truth and give credit where it is due.

Be Careful About Using Family Members in Illustrations
We all do this. Family experiences can be effective illustrations. This is especially true as we try to lend credibility to our illustrations by using firsthand experiences. But be careful. Don't tell stories that embarrass or betray confidences.

I told you it was simple! If this process doesn't work for you, find one that does. Effective illustrations will make your messages come alive.

20. (HOW TO) Develop an Annual Preaching Plan

Developing an annual preaching plan can be productive and rewarding. It can help you make the most of your sermon preparation time. It can give you the opportunity to look over your annual plan and recognize strengths and weaknesses. And developing an annual preaching plan is not only possible, but it's also simple.

Pray.—Of course, every preacher should pray as part of preparing every message. But I mean pray about the whole year. God knows what your people will face this year. He knows what passages should be presented and when each message should be preached. Do your best to discern the will of God about your preaching for the coming year.

A retreat-type setting is helpful.—If you are one of those preachers who can take a week away from the office and go to the mountains to plan your preaching, you are indeed blessed. I wish every preacher could do that. But if that is not possible for you, try to arrange some "retreat like" setting. Can you arrange a few days at a relative's home? Many seminaries offer low-cost, dormitory-type lodging and a great library. Perhaps a neighboring pastor could provide a comfortable Sunday School room where you would not be disturbed for a morning or two. A retreat doesn't have to mean a motel and lots of money. Find a way to invest yourself in your preaching plan. Explain to your people the purpose of this time and that you will be doing the hard work of planning sermons.

Prepare a file folder for each month of the year.—(See "19. How to File Sermon Illustrations.") Label 12 file folders with the 12 months of the year.

Take a look at the calendar.—There are lots of special days on the calendar when your sermon will, unless God clearly directs otherwise, be related to a seasonal emphasis. Certainly this is true of Christmas and Easter. Many pastors find benefit in relating messages to other special days such as Mother's Day, Independence day, etc. Put on paper the themes of those special days and a possible sermon focus. I usually use one sheet of paper for each month of the year. On the monthly sheet, I place the four or five

Sundays that will come during that month. If you need more space, use a sheet for each week. When the themes for special days are recorded, you may be surprised at how few Sundays remain.

Prayerfully consider sermons, series of sermons, passages, themes, or books of the Bible which you feel led to preach.—This planning process allows you to anticipate whether a five-sermon series will be interrupted by a special emphasis day. It also encourages you to take full advantage of the calendar. For example, between Mother's Day and Father's Day is an excellent time to preach a series of messages on the family. The seven Sundays before Easter may be a good time to preach on Jesus' statements from the cross.

Continue to develop the sermons for the coming year as much as time and resources allow.—If you get the main idea or theme down on paper, that will be of tremendous help. If you are able to develop each message more fully, that's even better. Even one morning invested in a preaching plan is valuable.

Constantly watch for illustrative material for the sermons you will preach.— Because you have invested the time to plan a year of sermons, God can bring those themes to your mind as you encounter illustrations. You may discover an illustration, early in the year, which perfectly fits a sermon you plan to preach in the fall. Since you have a plan and a file folder to house the plan, you will be able to find and use that illustration when preparing the sermon.

Be flexible.—Your annual preaching plan is prepared with prayer and careful attention. But God may choose to change your mind. The week of this writing, tornadoes ripped through a neighboring state. The pastors of churches in those communities certainly put aside their preaching plan and addressed the deep and immediate need of the people.

Preach the Word.—When you stand before God's people, open His Book and preach His message. Preach with clarity and confidence.

21. (HOW TO) Give an Effective Evangelistic Invitation

The sermon is ready. You have studied the text. Illustrations are in place. Your introduction will lead the congregation right into the truth God has placed on your heart for this Sunday. But is your preparation really complete?

What about the invitation? How will you transition from the conclusion of your sermon into the time of commitment? Here are a few tips that may be helpful.

Prepare spiritually.—God is surely dealing with someone who will hear your sermon. Certainly you will seek His guidance concerning the message. It is just as important to pray and seek His leadership about how the commitment opportunity will be presented.

Make the invitation clear.—Assume that people will be present who do not understand our Christian language. Even a child who is familiar with church talk may not really understand it. In fact, adults who have heard religious terms all their lives will find it easier to respond when clear, understandable language is used.

Tell people what they must know.—Near the conclusion of the message, restate the essential facts people must have to make an informed decision. If the message is evangelistic, state the essentials of salvation.

Tell people what action they should take.—If you want people to come forward during the singing of the invitation hymn and tell you about their decision or commitment, tell them so. Sometimes this is not as clear as we preachers think. For example, if the instrumentalists are playing softly, the newcomer may not know whether to come during this soft music or to wait for the choir to sing again. Tell them what they should say if they come forward and "take you by the hand." Be specific.

Tell people what will happen when they come forward.—Present your invitation as if you were preaching to people who have never before been in a church service. If you or someone will pray with them at the altar, tell

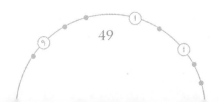

them so. If you will briefly greet them and someone else will take them to an inquiry room (be careful about using the terms *counseling* or *counselor*), tell them.

Give the invitation boldly.—Expect a response to the invitation. You are inviting people to Christ. You are inviting people to a renewed commitment to Him or to meaningful participation in His church. Clarify in your own thinking the invitation you are giving, then give it without hesitation or apology.

Prepare the people to expect and understand the invitation.—A public invitation to respond to Jesus is foreign to many who will hear your message. Make clear statements well in advance of actually offering the invitation. Consider a word of explanation in the bulletin or worship guide.

Use music appropriately during the invitation.—Use familiar hymns. This is not the time to learn a new text or tune. If choir or soloists are used, be sure it is done in a way that does not draw attention to the person or persons singing. Prearrange signals for quick, clear communication between you and the minister of music.

Invite people to pray at the altar.—Invite your people to come forward for prayer during the invitation. Unless you use an inquiry room, consider praying at the altar with those who come forward. If you use the altar, others will feel more free to pray there. (If you are a single staff pastor, be sure someone else is available to receive those who come forward while you are praying at the altar.)

Personalize the invitation.—People come to Christ one at a time. Speak as if you were speaking to one person about Jesus. Ask the audience to listen as though you were speaking directly and exclusively to them.

Adapted from Wayne Bristow, *Invitation to Christ* (Nashville: Convention Press, 1998).

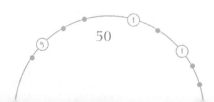

22. (HOW TO) Conduct a Funeral

The loss of a loved one is one of the most shocking and difficult experiences a person can encounter. It is a time when all Christians need the loving support of their pastor. Upon hearing of the death, the pastor should go immediately to the family and offer comfort and support. Be sensitive. Listen. Let them know that God cares and that you care.

Here are a few ideas to help as you minister through the funeral.

Make It Personal

When the funeral is for a church member, you will probably be well acquainted with the deceased. Even when this is the case, review the details of the obituary carefully. This is not the time for an inadvertent mispronunciation of a name or place of birth.

Do not use the funeral service to condemn the sins of the dead.

At an appropriate time (perhaps a second visit), ask the immediate family to help you prepare your comments for the memorial service. Ask, "What positive qualities come to mind when you think of _____?"

If the person who died was a faithful Christian, I ask to use their Bible in the funeral service. You may even find notes or passages underlined that will be significant.

Respect Local Traditions and Customs

The local funeral director can be of tremendous benefit to the pastor as he interprets local customs. Community traditions may dictate the order of service and even where the pastor should stand after the funeral. Don't hesitate to ask questions.

Be Professional

When you minister to a grieving family, you represent God and the church. Be caring and warm, but also communicate the quiet confidence of a professional who has been down this road and can serve as a guide.

Take Care of the Family

Sometimes a zealous pastor will, inadvertently I hope, deny family members permission to grieve. He says that since we will be together in heaven someday, there is no reason to grieve. But the reality of heaven does not erase the present pain death brings to a family. Paul said that Christians should "not grieve as others who have no hope" (1 Thes. 4:13). This is not a statement to deny grief; it is simply to say that Christians should grieve in a different manner.

Let the Powerful Word of God Bring Comfort

The Word of God is a powerful force for comfort in times of loss by death. Choose Scriptures that speak to the heart and communicate comfort. Claim the promises of Scripture. Apply the medicine of the Bible to grieving hearts.

Keep the Funeral Service Brief

A funeral service is an expression of the love of a family for the one who has died. The family is tired, and the funeral service gives them permission to begin the long journey to recovery. This is no time for a long, drawn-out service. A few well-planned comments will accomplish more than a long, rambling message.

Prepare for the Graveside Service

In most places the pastor should walk ahead of the casket from the hearse to the graveside. There the pastor should read a Scripture, offer a few words of comfort, and pray. Following his prayer, the pastor should say a personal word of comfort to the immediate family.

Make Follow-up Contacts After the Funeral

Don't forget to continue ministry after the funeral. During the stressful days of the funeral, life is busy, and lots of family members are usually nearby. Two weeks or a month after the funeral, things are quiet, and reality sets in. The wise pastor will realize that a contact from him may be more needed then than it was on the day of the death.

23. (HOW TO) Prepare for a Wedding

Regularly preach and teach on the Christian home, dating, etc.–Lay the ground-work for marriage in young people who grow up under your preaching.

Arrange a time for counseling the couple prior to the wedding.–During the counseling session, be sure to go through the plan of salvation. Invite the couple to affirm or make a commitment to Christ. Talk with the couple about the responsibilities they enter in marriage: finances, fulfillment in sexual relation-ships, planning for children, and the important relationship of home and church. Discuss the details of the wedding: music, rings, vows, rehearsal, etc.

Ensure that appropriate music is planned for the wedding service.–Ask the couple to give you copies of each piece to be sung. This practice can help you avoid embarrassing situations. Some music today is not appropriate for the church. Some music is so pagan that you would not even want to officiate at a wedding where it is used.

Conduct the wedding with dignity and rejoicing.–Be familiar with the service and plan for the wedding. Make notes to ensure that you will not forget or misstate a name or vow. Even though I never read a sermon, I still read wedding ceremonies. I then give the couple the copy of their ceremony from which I read.

Attend the wedding rehearsal.–It is usually held on the evening of the day before the wedding. The minister should direct the rehearsal. All members of the wedding party should be present. Begin with prayer that God will bless the rehearsal, the wedding, and the home to be established at the wedding.

At the wedding rehearsal, ask the wedding party to take their places on the platform.–(You will practice marching in later.) Invite someone to stand in for the bride and groom. With their help, get everyone set in just the right place. Then ask the instrumentalists to play the music to which the wedding party will leave the platform. Practice marching out. Then practice marching in, and go through the entire ceremony. (Don't actually pronounce them husband and wife. Save that for the next day.) Practice marching out again.

The following diagram may be useful in placing the wedding party on the platform.

53

THE WEDDING

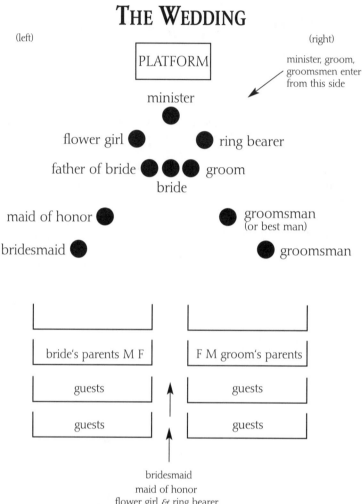

(left)   (right)

PLATFORM

minister, groom, groomsmen enter from this side

minister

flower girl   ring bearer

father of bride   groom

bride

maid of honor   groomsman
                                 (or best man)

bridesmaid   groomsman

bride's parents M F   F M groom's parents

guests   guests

guests   guests

bridesmaid
maid of honor
flower girl & ring bearer
father of bride & bride
enter from rear of auditorium

NOTES:

- Some prefer the best man and the maid of honor beside the bride and groom with the flower girl and ring bearer beside the bridesmaid and groomsman.
- Some prefer to place the father of the bride between the bride and groom until he is seated. Then the bride and groom come together.

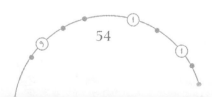

54

24. (HOW TO) Perform a Wedding

The wedding should be one of the most significant services in a person's life. It is a time for couples to make lifetime promises and express their love for each other. For believers, the wedding is a time to commit the family to God. As a pastor, you must do all you can to make the wedding service beautiful and meaningful for the couple and their friends and families. Here are a few principles.

Pave the way by preaching on God's ideal for marriage.–Nowhere else in society will your children and youth encounter the biblical standard for dating, marriage, and the Christian home. Preach the truth consistently and help prepare your people for marriage.

Set up a time for counseling before the wedding.–Consider such matters as the commitment and responsibility of marriage, finances, planning for children, and the important relationship of the home and church.[1] Also consider details of the wedding itself. (For more information see "23. How to Prepare for a Wedding.")

Discuss choices of music with the couple.–The wedding is a Christian service, and music should be appropriate.

Carefully plan the wedding ceremony and carry it out with joy and dignity.–As pastor, take the lead in this celebration of God's establishment of the home.

On the day of the wedding, the wedding party should arrive at least one hour before the ceremony is to begin.–Pictures will be made, clothing changed, and many last-minute details cared for. The organist or pianist should begin playing 15 minutes before the ceremony begins.

The parents of the groom will be seated by an usher about two minutes prior to the wedding time.–They are seated in the first pew at the right facing the pulpit.

The mother of the bride will be seated about one minute prior to the wedding time.–She will be seated in the first pew at the left.

If candle lighters are used, they may now light the candles.—Remember that some candles are difficult to light a second time and should not be lighted prior to the wedding.

A song may be sung prior to the processional.

The wedding party may now enter to appropriate music.—The following order is traditional.
• The minister enters from the right side when facing the pulpit.
• The groom and the groomsmen follow the minister.
• Bridesmaids enter the aisle singly. Each bridesmaid should wait until the other bridesmaid is halfway down the aisle before beginning.
• The maid of honor will enter, followed by the flower girl and ring bearer (if any).
• The bride and her father (or whoever gives her away) will enter, he walking on her right. When they approach the altar, the father will stand between the bride and groom for a brief time. When the minister asks, "Who gives this woman to be the wife of this man?" the father will answer, "Her mother and I," before taking his seat beside the mother of the bride.

The ceremony should include the following:
• Opening comments and prayer about marriage.
• Promises the couple make to each other. These are usually stated by the minister and answered with "I do."
• A statement by the minister about the significance of the rings and a ring vow.
• A pronouncement by the minister that the couple is now husband and wife.
• A prayer for the couple and their marriage.
• The kiss.

---

[1]Larry Burkett, *Money in Marriage. A Biblical Approach* (Moody Press Edition, 1999)

25. (HOW TO) Plan More Meaningful Worship Experiences

Worship is an encounter with God. Any time we come into His presence, worship takes place. When God's people gather for a "worship service," we as leaders have the opportunity to lead them to worship, that is, lead them into the presence of God. Here are a few ideas I find helpful in planning meaningful worship experiences.

Pray.—As a pastor, you would not think of preaching without spending much time in prayer. Just as preaching is important enough to deserve prayer time, so is all the worship time. Spend quality time seeking the will of God concerning each worship service. Whether you are a single-staff pastor or leader of a staff team, you as pastor should lead the way in prayer.

Plan well; be intentional.—In my earliest years as a pastor, I would take last week's bulletin, white out the hymn numbers, type in some new ones, and call that worship planning. It was not. Intentional planning means developing the entire service around a theme. It means giving time and attention to all the details of the worship service.

Plan something fresh for each week.—You know that moment in a worship time when something fresh happens and the participants experience that warm, genuine sense of the presence of God. Perhaps the fresh moment comes when a simple, sincere prayer touches hearts. It may come as a child reads Scripture or when a chorus is tagged unexpectedly to a familiar hymn. If you announce the name and number of the chorus, it's not fresh. Just sing it. For example, add the first verse of "Amazing Grace" to the end of "Nothing but the Blood." If you announce the name and number of "Amazing Grace," it is just another hymn. But if you just go into it, it is a fresh moment. If you pray about each service, God will give you one fresh moment for each service.

Enhance corporate prayer times.—Praying during a worship service is different from private prayer time. Prayer during a worship service is a conversation with God, but it is not a private conversation. The one who leads in public prayer speaks, in a sense, for the entire congregation. While you cannot provide a scripted prayer for those who lead in corporate prayer, you can attempt to improve corporate prayer in your services.

- Train deacons to lead in public prayer.
- Ask all worship leaders (including those who will lead in prayer) to gather for prayer before the worship service. In a sentence or two, interpret the focus of the worship time for that day. Encourage those who will lead in prayer to address the theme in their prayers.
- Use a Sunday or Wednesday night to teach your people about corporate prayer.

None of these ideas will completely solve the problem, but each of them will help.

Make giving time meaningful.—Giving is an act of worship. It is not just a time of collecting money.

- Train ushers to give all worshipers the opportunity to participate by holding the offering plate even if they have already given during Sunday School.
- Talk to your people about giving as an act of worship. Remind them of this just before the offering is given.
- Consider leading the congregation to read a "worship passage" aloud together just before receiving the offering. Print the passage in the bulletin.

Eliminate dead time.—Ask all those who will speak or lead to come to the platform before their appointed time and be ready to begin without delay when their time comes. Most introductions are unnecessary if you use a bulletin or worship guide.

Strive for excellence.—This Sunday your congregation will gather at the house of God. They will come with all kinds of needs. The one thing they will all have in common is a need to encounter God. Let no unattended detail or poorly planned moment stand in the way. Regardless of the worship style you find comfortable, strive for excellence in everything you do.

26. (HOW TO) Work with Your Minister of Music to Plan Effective Worship

Plan the services together.—No one person has all the answers as to what a worship service should be. Put your best thinking and ideas on the worship-planning table. Let them commingle with ideas from other people. Remember, the worship service is not to be a showcase for the creativity of a human leader but rather a time when God is allowed to speak and manifest Himself in any number of ways.

If you cannot plan together, at least tell the minister of music what you're going to preach.—This comment is almost always in first place on the list of expectations music leaders have of their pastors. While nearly every church music leader can recount numerous times when he had to plan blindly for a service with no clue as to the sermon topic or theme, he has also marveled at how the Holy Spirit has merged the efforts of the pastor and music director into one spiritually moving and unified service. "If God can bless our efforts with little or no planning, how much more could He bless us with even a little planning in our shared worship experience?" more than one music director has asked.

Allow the minister of music lead time to prepare for Sunday services.—The pastor has only himself to prepare for church on Sunday. Music leaders, however, have numerous other persons to get ready for their involvement in the worship service. These others may range from the choir to soloists, from instrumentalists to sound and light technicians, and from dramatists to ensembles. Give your music leaders as much lead time as you possibly can.

Encourage your minister of music to take advantage of training opportunities.—Some who direct the music on Sunday morning do so at the request of the pastor with no formal training. Reward their willingness. Few volunteer music leaders can afford to take time away from their vocations and spend their own limited funds to secure training on their own. But with encouragement from the pastor and the church providing the funds, most volunteer leaders will agree to take some training.

Whether the music leader in a church is paid or unpaid, everyone likes to be appreciated.–Commend the minister of music when praise is deserved; offer redirection when the quality is not what it should be. An occasional good word, pat on the back, and public recognition provide affirmation for every worker. The pastor's leadership in these areas is important.

Help the minister of music to identify traditional church music practices and customs and not to make hasty decisions regarding change.–It's sometimes difficult for a minister of music, new to a church, to recognize quickly traditional church music practices and customs within a congregation.

Communicate your goals and desires for the church as a whole as well as your work habits and preferences.–Sometimes the minister of music feels kept in the dark about your preferences and sense of direction. Share confidentially. Pray and share spiritual moments together. Remember that the minister of music is a member of your team and desires to support you, as the spiritual leader of the church, in every way possible.

Adapted from the writings of Danny R. Jones, manager, Adult Enrichment Events, Central Operations, LifeWay Church Resources, Nashville, Tennessee.

Resource

Let's Worship is a 96-page quarterly magazine published by LifeWay Church Resources to help pastors and other worship leaders in planning, guiding, and facilitating corporate worship.

27. (HOW TO) Involve Children in Worship

Too often children are expected to experience genuine worship even though the worship service is designed completely for adults. You and I are much more likely to worship when we are participants in worship, not just observers. The same is true for children. Here are a few ways to involve children in worship.

Schedule an Invitation to Worship meeting involving parents and children.— Promote the meeting in children's and parent's Sunday School classes, the church newsletter and bulletin, and other ministries that touch children or their parents. Use the meeting to accomplish three things.

1. Discuss ways to help children really experience God in worship. Use the ideas uncovered during this meeting throughout the year.
2. Educate parents about the importance of worship for their children. Enlist their support and help in involving children in worship.
3. Encourage family worship times.

Use these ideas to involve children in worship.

- Ask children to read Scripture during a worship service. Be sure to choose children that are ready to do this. Avoid situations that might embarrass a child.
- Ask children to lead the congregation in prayer. Ask the child well in advance. Help the parents prepare the child for this responsibility.
- Enlist and train children to receive the offering from time to time. It may be helpful to enlist adults to participate alongside the children.
- Preach a children's sermon. This might be a regular feature in which you as pastor share a lesson designed especially for children. It might also be a way of presenting the sermon with a special focus for children.
- Calendar a Sunday as Children's Day. Recognize children in the morning worship service, and invite children and families to a church-sponsored picnic that afternoon. Be sure you, as pastor, attend and participate. The children need to get to know you in an informal setting.
- Consider using a listening sheet for children in worship. You may choose to give children a small reward if they show you the completed listening sheet following the service. Here is a low-tech sample.

My name is _____.

I am sitting in church with _____.

The song we sang in church that I liked best was _____

_____.

The special music this morning was _____

_____.

The Scripture reading this morning was:

book _____ chapter _____verse _____.

The name of the person who led in prayer was _____

_____.

Here is one thing the pastor said _____

_____.

- Ask the adult choir or an adult who sings a special to sing a children's song and dedicate it to the children in the worship service.
- Invite the children's choir to sing during the morning worship service.
- Ask a child to play a musical instrument as part of a praise time.
- Involve children's missions organizations by asking them to provide a missions moment during the worship service. This feature should present or interpret some missionary person or ministry to the congregation.
- Invite a child to give a personal testimony entitled, "I'm Glad I'm a Christian Because. . . ."

Adapted from Rosey Davis, "Involving Children in Worship," *Church Administration* (December 1989), 22–23.

Resource

For more helps with children's pages, see *Let's Worship,* a 96-page quarterly magazine published by LifeWay Church Resources to help pastors and other worship leaders in planning, guiding, and facilitating corporate worship.

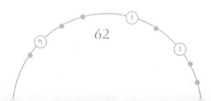

28. ⬤ HOW TO Introduce Drama into the Worship of a Traditional Church

Drama, for the most part, requires a little planning; but doesn't everything worth its salt? Here are 10 simple, easy, and inexpensive ways to make dramatic changes in your church.

1. Instead of simply having one person read the Scripture, have two or three people divide the Scriptures into parts and read it. For instance, read the story of Adam and Eve, using a narrator, someone reading Adam's words, another reading Eve's, another reading the serpent's, and one reading God's lines.

2. Have someone learn American Sign Language interpretation for a familiar hymn and sign the words as the congregation sings. There's a good chance someone in your congregation already knows sign language and would love to help you with this.

3. Allow your youth to act out one of their favorite Christian songs. They will enjoy doing this, and you'll be surprised by their insight and creativity. Be sure to give them some adult supervision.

4. Consider a subscription to the *National Drama Service*. Available on the Dated Materials Order Forms or by subscription. This quarterly publication of 20-25 scripts gives you photocopy rights to all the material. Most of the scripts require limited props and lighting. They are short enough to be incorporated into a traditional worship gathering. Drama is a regular feature in *Let's Worship* magazine. To order call, 1-800-458-2772.

5. Preach through the beatitudes and have teams of youth or adults assigned to improvise a situation that illustrates a certain beatitude. Give each team a few weeks' notice; and if you keep encouraging them, you'll be surprised what they might create! (This would work with many other series, such as the phrases of the Lord's Prayer, the parables, and others.)

6. Use sound effects during Scripture readings. Sound effects tapes are easily found in most music stores. Imagine reading the parable of the wise and foolish builder with the sounds of construction and then sounds of a coming storm!

7. Candles can add drama to any service. Try turning the lights off, lighting a candle, and reading the following monologue:

This Little Light of Mine

We loved the light, so we built a church around it to shelter it
    from the cold, dark world.
And every Monday night we take it out to visit those who saw
    he light last Sunday.
We have matchbooks we carry with us, but we're afraid to use
    them for fear that something might catch fire and we
    wouldn't be able to control it.
So we leave the candle at the church where we can visit it
    whenever we want.
We love our light, but it seems these days that the light is
    getting dim—perhaps because it's running out of oxygen
    due to the walls we've built around it.
Every now and then I wonder what would happen if we
    opened the door and let the fire warm and the light shine,
    but we've grown quite accustomed to the darkness.
Hide it under a bushel? No!
We'd much prefer hiding it in a church.
We know Satan would never find it there; would he?
(Pause, next line to be sung)
Don't let Satan—
(Blow the candle out).

8. Use Readers Theater. It's easy and nonthreatening to untrained
dramatists. It requires rehearsal, familiarity, and expression; but it
doesn't require memorization. For a wealth of readers material, let
me recommend *The Imaginary Stage* (Church Street Press). This is a
book of easy-to-do Readers Theater sketches.

9. Read the famous poem "Touch of the Master's Hand." Hold a violin
as you read about the auction, then have a violinist come out of the
audience and play as you read the concluding verses of the poem.

10. Encourage artistic members to express their gift in the life of your
church. For some it will be storytelling, painting, song writing,
acting, or clowning. For others it may be simply a concept that
someone else may be able to interpret. One thing is certain: If you
open the door for drama, done with excellence and creativity, it will
breathe new vitality and vision to whatever church you are serving.

Matt Tullos is Editor-in-Chief of *The Deacon* and *The Minister's Family* magazines, LifeWay Church Resources, Nashville, Tennessee.

Resource

Let's Worship is a 96-page quarterly magazine published by LifeWay Church
Resources to help pastors and other worship leaders in planning, guiding,
and facilitating corporate worship.

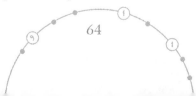

29. ⬤HOW TO Baptize

Baptism should be a beautiful and meaningful experience for both the one baptized and the entire congregation. Here are a few tips to help make the baptismal service a memorable worship experience.

Always be intentional and worshipful in your approach to this ordinance.– Make it special.

Always give baptismal candidates an opportunity to share their new birth experience with you before you baptize them.–In a comfortable setting, away from the pressure or nervousness of a public testimony, allow them to tell their pastor about inviting Jesus to be Lord and Master. It is a tragedy when persons make an insincere profession and go through years with a false sense of confidence because they have been baptized. If the testimony is unclear, take the opportunity to lead them through a clear profession right then. Explain that you love them and want them to have complete confidence, in the years to come, that their decision was valid. Most will appreciate the opportunity to nail down this life-changing decision.

Invite family and friends of baptismal candidates to the baptismal service.– The baptismal service presents a wonderful opportunity for testimony. Prepare a special letter from the pastor inviting friends of the person to be baptized. Ask the candidate to provide names of family and friends to be invited.

In a prebaptism session, explain the beautiful symbolism of baptism.– Most people think baptism only pictures the washing away of sins. Remind them that it is also a picture of the death, burial, and resurrection of Christ. Explain that when they go under the water the end of the old life is pictured and as they come up out of the water it is a picture of the beginning of new life in Christ. Ask them to focus their thoughts on these beautiful pictures during the baptism itself.

During the prebaptism session, explain the mechanics of the baptismal service.–Many new believers have never seen a person baptized. Show them the baptismal pool. Explain how and where they should stand and how they should position their hands. Some pastors prefer that the candidate fold his or her hands together at about chest height. Others ask the candidate to grasp the wrist of the pastor.

As the person to be baptized stands in the water with the pastor, ask those who are family and friends of the person to stand.—Then invite others in the congregation to stand with the person. As these are standing, lead a special prayer for this person. Invite the congregation to be seated.

Place your left hand on the back or shoulder of the person to be baptized.—Ask the person to grasp the wrist of your right hand.

Ask the person to bend his or her knees as you lower the person into the water.—Pause for a second (literally) just as the person's back is floating on the surface of the water. Just before the person is immersed, gently close their nostrils with your fingers (some prefer a clean handkerchief covering the mouth and nose). Lower the person just until the face is under the water. Then gently raise the person out of the water.

Some pastors quote an appropriate Scripture as the person is immersed and raised.—For example, you might say, "Buried with Him by baptism unto death," as you lower the person, and, "Raised to walk in newness of life," as you raise the person from the water.

Rick White, senior pastor, First Baptist Church, Franklin, Tennessee, gives each person a lighted candle before they leave the baptistry. He touches his finger to a bowl of salt, then to the lips of the one just baptized. As they leave the baptistery, he says, "You are the light of the world; you are the salt of the earth."

30. (HOW TO) Lead an Effective Lord's Supper Observance

Observance of the Lord's Supper should be one of the most significant and meaningful worship experiences for the church. To worship in this manner fulfills the command of Jesus and follows the example of the New Testament church. The observance of the Lord's Supper is worthy of your most prayerful planning. Here are a few ideas.

Make the Lord's Supper the focus of the entire service.—To tack it onto the end of a service is to trivialize something sacred.

Use a variety of approaches.—Take advantage of excellent resources like *Proclaim* and *Let's Worship*. Find ideas to keep the worship experience fresh. Consider inviting the congregation to come forward by families and receive the elements. Have a candlelight Lord's Supper observance at Christmas. Have the Lord's Supper in the fellowship hall, around tables, and pass elements around the tables, perhaps even using a loaf of unleavened bread from which each person pulls a small piece.

Preach sermons that prepare people for the Lord's Supper.—Two brief messages on the body and blood may be incorporated into the observance. A message on the Old Testament observance of Passover or the sacrificial system in the Old Testament is appropriate. Sermons from the New Testament passages on the Lord's Supper are always meaningful (see 1 Cor. 11; Mark 14; Matt. 26; Luke 22).

Involve lots of people in the observance.—A committee of deacons or their wives should prepare the elements. Individuals may sing, read Scriptures, or lead in prayer. In most churches it is the custom that deacons serve the elements and a minister preside.

Use music to help lead the people into this experience of worship.—Have a choir, small group, or soloist sing as the elements are passed.

Ask the deacons and others involved in leading the service to gather for a few minutes of prayer and final preparation before the Lord's Supper begins.— Make sure everyone understands where to stand, when to pass the elements, and when prayers are to take place. A diagram of the auditorium with assignments may be helpful.

Enlist enough deacons to serve the elements in a reasonable amount of time.—It may help to start one group serving from the back to the front while another group serves from the front to the back.

Lord's Supper Observance
1. Pastor takes his place behind the Lord's Supper table.
2. Two deacons (one probably the chairman) take places at each end of the table and fold the cover and put it aside.
3. Deacons stand and take their places. (I like them to stand, half on each side of the table, facing the congregation.)
4. Pastor reads 1 Corinthians 11: 23-24.
5. Pastor distributes the bread trays to the deacons.
6. One of the deacons leads in prayer.
7. Deacons serve the bread to the congregation.
8. When all are served, deacons return to their places beside the table.
9. Pastor serves deacons, and deacon chairman serves pastor.
10. Pastor says, "Jesus said, 'This is my body which is broken for you. This do in remembrance of me.'" Then all partake of bread together.
11. Pastor reads 1 Corinthians 11:25.
12. Pastor distributes juice trays to deacons.
13. One of the deacons leads in prayer.
14. Deacons will serve the juice to the congregation.
15. When all are served, deacons return to their places beside the table.
16. Pastor serves deacons; deacon chairman serves pastor.
17. Pastor says, "Jesus said, 'This is my blood which is shed for you. Do this in remembrance of me.'" Then all will drink the juice together.
18. The entire congregation may sing an appropriate hymn.

31. (HOW TO) Lead an Effective Parent-Child Dedication Service

Few things in life bring more joy than the birth of a child. Many times, during my 18 years as a pastor, parents requested that I baptize their child. These parents usually came from a nonevangelical background. I explained that we Baptists believe that baptism should take place only after a person personally receives Jesus as Lord and Savior. Therefore, we don't baptize babies. But the question always brought with it a chance to witness to new parents about Jesus, our church, and the value of a Christian home. Many times, the parents just wanted some way to thank God for their child, ask His blessing on their home, and dedicate their family to Him. Of course, most born-again couples who have a new baby are eager to dedicate themselves and the child to the Lord.

A Parent-Child Dedication Service is one good way to satisfy this need and worship God. I have intentionally chosen the title "Parent-Child Dedication Service" for this event. It is more than a "baby dedication." The parents should think of the service as an opportunity to dedicate themselves as well. Here are a few tips and some ideas for a service.

Make it personal.—Call the parents by name. Call the child by name. Pray for the parents and children by name. Present a gift, such as a Bible, to the child.

At least once a year, offer parents of children up to five years old an opportunity to participate.—Although this service may be for a newborn baby, others may appreciate an opportunity to dedicate themselves and their child.

One good model for the dedication is to focus on the family and home for the entire service.—The month of May is an ideal time for this. The Parent-Child Dedication can become an annual event in your church. Contact all members who have given birth in the last year and invite them to participate.

Another approach is to take a moment to recognize and dedicate during the first service the new baby attends.—In our church, we always know a new

69

baby is present when we see a single rose in a vase on the pulpit. The pastor introduces the family, including the new baby. The child is presented a Bible, and the entire congregation joins in a prayer of dedication.

Consider a responsive reading.—One approach is to ask the parents a set of questions to which the parents answer, "We do." You will probably want to write your own, but here are a few ideas for the covenant.

> **Pastor to parents:** Do you desire that your child will grow in the fear and admonition of the Lord, and do you promise to provide for _____ (insert the child's first name) a Christian home where God is honored and His word is taught?
> **Parents:** We do.
> **Pastor to parents:** Do you pledge yourselves to live in such a way that your words and actions will commend Jesus and His church to your child?
> **Parents:** We do.
> **Pastor to parents:** Do you promise that you will be for _____ a spiritual guide, praying and watching for the day when your child will be ready to receive Christ as personal Lord and Savior?
> **Parents:** We do.
> **Pastor to congregation:** Do you, the people of God in this church, covenant with these parents to provide a loving church home for _____?
> **Congregation:** We do.
> **Pastor to congregation:** Do you promise to continue teaching the Bible in this church, so that this child will never lack hearing the truth of God's Word?
> **Congregation:** We do.

Consider making a presentation to the child or family.—A Bible, a rose, a book, or even a picture (presented after the service) are appropriate.

Conclude with a prayer of dedication.—Make it personal and simple.

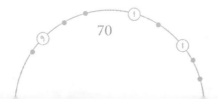

32. (HOW TO) Overcome Discouragement

When you get up early on a cold, winter morning and go look at the fireplace, it seems that the fire is out. The ashes are gray and cold. But if you take a stick and dig around in those ashes, you will discover red-hot coals. With proper care, you can rekindle the fire that seemed to be gone.

This is the word picture Paul painted for Timothy when he said, "Kindle afresh the gift of God which is in you" (2 Tim. 1:6, NASB). Paul pictured Timothy's pastoral gift as a fire that once blazed brightly but had almost gone out. Underneath the dull, gray ashes were still hot coals, capable of bursting into flames again, if they were stirred.

Pastors today face the same challenge. There are three things every pastor can do to overcome discouragement and rekindle his enthusiasm.

Remember the Lay of the Harvest

Paul said, "Let us not be weary in well doing for in due season we shall reap, if we faint not" (Gal. 6:9). The law of the harvest says if you keep planting good seed in good soil in God's time there will be fruit.

Not all fields are equally productive. You may be serving in a difficult place. The people around you may be hardened and callused. We are to work hard no matter where we are, no matter how great or little the harvest may be. Our task is to be faithful to God, to plant good seed in the soil around us, and to let God handle the amount and quality of the harvest.

Use the Right Standard to Evaluate Your Work

How do you measure success in the kingdom of God? If you attend a convention and a friend asks how your church is doing, would your answer be numerical and include nothing else?

The healthy church is reaching people for Christ and teaching them the Bible. However, in some churches great numerical increase is unlikely. All church fields are not equally productive. Do not measure success by comparing yourself to other pastors and churches. To do so only creates a sense of pride if you do better than they or jealousy, envy, and despair if you do worse.

Success in the kingdom of God is measured by faithfulness. Don't compare yourself to others.

Trust in God

He is still on the throne. The work you do as a pastor is kingdom work–God's kingdom. Depend on God for the strength to overcome discouragement. In 1 John 5:4, John said, "This is the victory that overcomes the world, even our faith."

Discouragement is a powerful tool for Satan. He uses it to immobilize God's pastors. But God is still God, and we are still His servants. Depend on Him for strength and encouragement. You are an overcomer.

Adapted from Paul Powell, *Shepherding the Sheep in Smaller Churches* (Dallas: Annuity Board of the Southern Baptist Convention, 1995), 79-90.

33. HOW TO Recognize and Recover from Burnout

Burnout is when you are completely empty. You are spiritually, physically, and emotionally poured out. There is nothing left to offer. Not surprisingly, this condition is common in pastors. In fact, we all have experienced some degree of burnout. If, however, you are consistently or persistently empty and would describe your condition as burnout, you are in danger. Here are some ways to recognize burnout.

Ten Danger Signals
1. Your devotional life is suffering.
2. Your family life is being adversely affected.
3. You have a nagging sense of ever being behind.
4. You find yourself with a low threshold for inconvenience.
5. Sabbath rest is the exception rather than the norm.
6. You experience a sense of overall weariness.
7. Physical exercise is sporadic or nonexistent.
8. Physical ailments are increasing.
9. The sense of serving God with gladness is gone.
10. You fight periodic thoughts of fleeing from the will of God.

   If any of the conditions listed above is consistently present in your life, you need help. Talk to a friend or a trusted associate. Even though it is important that you not try to bear all this burden alone, here are some tips to help you emerge from burnout.

Ten Insights
1. Wait on God as a necessity, not a nicety.
2. See the home as the launching pad for all public ministry.
3. Recognize the need for supportive relationships.
4. Remember that character must precede charisma.
5. Commit yourself to build for permanence.
6. Learn to plan, delegate, and manage your time.
7. Plan time off carefully and creatively.
. Be released to say no.

9. Make exercise and proper nutrition an integral part of your life.
10. Stay in your "sphere" and resist the snare of comparison.

The Road to Recovery

1. Confess to God: "I can't!" Let yourself off the hook. Don't beat yourself up.
2. Embrace the pain. Don't fight it (Rom. 5:1-5).
3. Everything that happens can be used of God to prepare and strengthen you (Rom. 8:28).
4. Find a safe environment in which to share your feelings on a regular basis. Feelings will express themselves eventually. Choose to express them in healthy, voluntary ways. Don't wait for them to erupt in emotional outbursts, burnout, and physical ailments.
5. Find a trusted support group or a compassionate counselor who knows how to listen without giving foolish and unwanted advice. Discipline yourself to share weekly with this person. Pray together. Let this person share positive insights when you can see only the negatives.
6. Learn not to share with wounders. Some will use information you share to hurt you.
7. Feed your weakened spirit. Include books, tapes, recreation, heroes.
8. When you can't praise God, be honest. God desires "truth in the inward parts" (Ps. 51:6).
9. Take time for fun.
10. Eat nutritionally balanced meals and rest.
11. Stop violating the Sabbath rest principle. It may be impossible for you to rest on Sunday, but you need a day of rest sometime during the week.

The LeaderCare ministry of the LifeWay Church Resources has a hotline for pastors, staff members, and their families. If you are suffering from burnout, give them a call at 1-888-789-9111. Someone will be there to listen and provide guidance as you move through this pilgrimage.

Adapted from Larry Tomczak, *Burnout or Burn-On.*

34. (HOW TO) Exercise

It does make a difference! Exercise:
- Enhances a sense of total well-being. It will improve your mental outlook, and you will feel better.
- Burns extra calories—not only during the exercise itself but also throughout the day. Physical activity tends to keep your metabolic rate (rate at which your body functions and uses calories) higher throughout the day.
- Creates efficient heartbeats. Your heart will become much more efficient with more blood being pumped at each beat, thereby decreasing beats per minute.
- Reduces stress level. Movement of large muscles through exercise reduces muscle tension, thereby improving relaxation while improving alertness to undertake challenges.
- Increases creativity. The flow of oxygen is improved. Tired minds become refreshed.
- Improves concentration. Making exercise a part of your everyday routine is one of the best ways to get a fresh start.
- Stops worry. Exercise eases the mind, slows worry, allows for a new perspective.
- Exchanges quality of life for chances of disease. Exercise reduces the risk of many diseases (e.g., some cancers, heart attack, stroke, high blood pressure, adult-onset diabetes).

Walking

It's easy to do. No special equipment is needed beyond a comfortable pair of shoes; and it is an anywhere, anytime activity—indoors or outdoors, malls, gymnasiums, neighborhoods, airports, hallways. It can be done alone or with a partner. It is safe, low impact, and provides many health benefits.

Pick a time.—"If you can think it, ink it." Schedule that time just like any other appointment and respect it just like any appointment.

Having difficult scheduling a time? Look for small spots to include. For instance, walk three to five minutes before coffee break or three to five minutes before lunch, three to five minutes after lunch, three to five minutes before and after the evening meal. Walk the long way when you do hospital visitation. Invite someone to walk with you as you discuss a problem or a new idea.

Pick a course.—Decide where you will walk. You may start in your neighborhood, but just start.

Pick a pace.—The important element here is to increase the rate at which you normally breathe and increase your heart rate without overdoing it. You should not exercise at an intensity that you are totally breathless and cannot converse with another person.

Ten Things to Do While Walking
1. Admire what is around you.
2. Memorize Scripture.
3. Pray. After all, it is the posture of your spirit, not your body, that is important.
4. Plan your day or the next day.
5. Evaluate your work to that point in the day.
6. Just daydream.
7. Count your blessings. Take time to name how God has blessed you.
8. Recount what you've done. Name what God has done through you in the past year, three years, five years, total ministry.
9. Think of something creative.
10. Listen to what is going on around you.

By Tommy Yessick, Minister's Wellness, Recreation and Sports Ministry Specialist, Ministry Team Leadership Department, LifeWay Church Resources, Nashville, Tennessee.

35. (HOW TO) Nurture Emotional Well-being

In *The Deadly Emotions*, Ernest H. Johnson presented the role of anger, hostility, and aggression in cancer, ulcers, and psoriasis, not to exclude cardiovascular disease on the physical side and martial problems and abuse in the social realm.[1] Given this, it would seem that to nurture your emotional health would be worth it, don't you think? Let's look at some things to nurture your immune system through your emotional well-being.

Feelings

You have them, so you might as well use them—correctly. The appropriate expression of the basic emotions of glad, sad, mad, and scared will be a gigantic step toward nurture of healthy emotions as well as reducing stress.

Glad.—Be willing to share your gladness and allow others to share their gladness with you. Taking a genuine interest in the gladness and successes of others will help with yours. This will require active listening on your part. You can do it by focusing on what the other person is saying, not what you want to say or wish you were doing.

Well, this is good, but it's not helping me, you may think. Yes, it is. As you discover the gladness in others, you should be able to pass on your gladness.

Sad.—A less than positive emotion such as sadness may not be as easy to express. Nonetheless it needs to be dealt with on an ongoing basis. The withholding and storing up of your sadness can only lead to problems. No matter what triggers the feelings of sadness, unhappiness, sorrow, or gloom, don't keep it to your self. Tell one or two of your closest, most trusted friends of your sadness. Your burden will not be as heavy when you allow someone else to know.

Mad.—Anger, or rage, can eat you alive from the inside out. Left unchecked it will explode on the scene at an inopportune time or at an unsuspecting and undeserving person. Anger, especially as it gives way to hostility, can contribute to your ill health and likelihood of disease. You're mad? If you're real mad, or even a little mad, pause a few moments for a reality check. Then discuss your anger with another person. This is best if the person is involved in the anger-causing situation. If you can't do that or no one is around to talk it out, then do a simple activity to help. Take a walk, preferably outside and for at least 15 minutes. The moving around will help keep the anger from building and will help you gain a different perspective.

Scared (alarmed, frightened, or anxious).—Most people, especially men, don't want to deal with being frightened. If you're scared of something, let it be known to your spouse or a good friend. Include doubt or uncertainty of a decision. You might be nervous about moving, starting a new program, or dealing with a difficult situation in your church or family. By talking it out with one or two well-chosen people, you might find out how realistic your concern is. The other person can provide insight to making a realistic assessment of the situation.

Laughter

The shortest distance between two people is a smile. Laughter is internal jogging. It changes the physiology of the cell. You increase antibodies, relax muscles, reduce blood pressure, release immune boosters, and improve ventilation.

Nurture your laughter/sense of humor. Try these ideas:
- List people you like to be around, those who are funny.
- Look for humorous signs around you or just the humorous placement of signs.
- Pay attention to what children say and ask. You're bound to hear things that will make you smile.
- Keep a humor file—a collection of funny saying, cartoons, or stories you can pull out and read.

Your emotional well-being is at the base of the way you approach life on a day-to-day basis. It is a filter and safety net. It can give you the stability to function whatever the situation. Work on it, share it, give it a chance.

By Tommy Yessick, Minister's Wellness, Recreation and Sports Ministry Specialist, Ministry Team Leadership Department, LifeWay Church Resources, Nashville, Tennessee.

[1]Ernest H. Johnson, *The Deadly Emotions: The Role of Anger, Hostility and Aggression in Health and Emotional Well-Being* (Westport, CT: Greenwood Publishing Group, 1990).

36. (HOW TO) Grow Your Intellectual Well-being

Intellectual well-being relates to your mental capacity, your ability to learn, and your ability to use your God-given mind to a fuller extent. The challenge is to use more than the 10–15 percent of your mind that we are told we use. How do you do this?

Learn

Your brain has thousands of cells and neurons which process and connect tremendous amounts of information. Your brain is more than some mere computer. It has the ability to reason, factor in more than just facts, produce options, and change course. "Wise men store up knowledge" (Prov. 10:14). "For as he thinks within himself, so he is" (Prov. 23:7, NASB).

Learning is a matter that goes beyond a school diploma. It is continuing to learn throughout life. You may say, "I don't have time," but you do! You learn all the time. Do you not read the paper, check on the news, or find out who won a ball game? Do you not check on a church member's physical condition? Yes, you are in the learning mode. So expand the idea of learning.

Read something different, maybe even a kid's book, maybe even read a little to your kids or a group of kids.

Go to a museum.

Watch an educational program, not just a mind-numbing TV show. Try a few minutes of the Discovery Channel or your public broadcasting station.

Ask honest, interested questions about someone else's work. Find out how something is done or why it is done that way.

Listen to a book on tape while you drive.

Hardiness

Hardiness is the attitude that you can make difference in your area. It does make a difference that you are where God put you. Your work is changing the lives of others. It may not be as fast as you like. It may not be as many as you like. It may not be a often as you like. But you are making a difference.

It is commitment to your work. You may call it a "call." This sense of call and commitment is what gets you through the rough times. Knowing you are doing God's work, in the right place, at the right time will provide strength and encouragement.

It is approaching life as a challenge and not a threat. Yes, you are going to fail sometimes, but a chance to succeed is there also—the chance to make a difference. The challenge is examining the small ways to move toward your ultimate goal, project, or program.

"Truth" Thinking

This is more than just positive thinking. It is knowing what is true and using that to support your attitude. Truths of the Scripture are a good place to start.

- Know that you are in God's loving care—now and forever.
- Determine to trust God. Give it more than just lip service.
- Know that God can heal your hurts and illness.
- Know that the past is the past. Learn from it, but don't live in it (see Phil 3:13).
- Know, as a sense of courage and optimism, that you can do all things through Christ, who is your source of strength (see Phil. 4:13).
- Determine to love others unconditionally. Accept them as they are. God does the changing.
- Determine to accept the assurance that God is with you all the time.

Make these basic ideas of truth part of the fabric of your life. It will change your intellectual well-being.

By Tommy Yessick, Minister's Wellness, Recreation and Sports Ministry Specialist, Ministry Team Leadership Department, LifeWay Church Resources, Nashville, Tennessee.

37. (HOW TO) Keep Your Physical Well-being

Physical well-being includes the awareness and practice of behaviors regarding exercise. It also includes your practices in nutrition, medical self-care, and safety. Your choices in these areas will add quality and length to your life.

Exercise.—Physical activity impacts every system of your body. The equivalent of 30–45 minutes of walking 4–6 times a week greatly diminishes your chances of death by disease. Regular physical activity can boost quality and quantity of life. Relatively small changes in the life of the nonexerciser can bring about drastic improvement. It does this by:

• Reducing the risk of heart attack, stroke, high blood pressure, kidney failure, adult-onset diabetes, and some cancers.
• Improving joint function.
• Making stronger bones.
• Improving muscle strength and flexibility.
• Resulting in less depression.
• Improving sense of well-being.
• Offering better weight control.
• Boosting your immune system.

Nutrition.—What you eat affects the cells of your body for 48–72 hours. The awareness of effect of nutrition on your health continues to grow. Two basic premises are essential:

1. No one needs to go on a diet; they need to change their diet.—People approach diets as a short-term plan to bring about a desired outcome, usually weight loss. One's short-term diet is abandoned at the point of goal achieved or an "it's not worth it" attitude. Ninety-five percent of those who lose the weight regain it because they are off the diet. The change in the way you eat over the long haul will make the lasting difference not just in weight but in overall health. It does not mean you cannot have some of your favorite foods, at times, which leads to the next premise.

2. You can eat some of what you want, if you eat all of what you need.—When you examine the food pyramid, this become clearer.

Here are some helpful, healthful hints on nutrition:

• Eat at least five servings of fruits and vegetables per day. The American Institute for Cancer Research estimates that if every person in America would eat a total of five servings of fruits and vegetables per day

incidences of cancer would be reduced by 20 percent.
- Reduce saturated fats by choosing the leanest meats and removing any fat prior to cooking, using low-fat and no-fat dairy products, and eliminating palm and coconut oil from foods you eat.
- Drink plenty of water and fruit juice, six to eight glasses per day. (Fruit drinks, which tend to be high in sugars, and soft drinks, coffee, and tea do not count as water.)
- Consume carbohydrates including whole-grain products, pastas, rice, legumes, fruits, and vegetables.

Medical self-care.—You can help yourself and your family.
- Learn the early warning signs for prostate and colon cancer.
- Find-out about hypoglycemia and adult-onset diabetes.
- Get a regular physical examination. Early detection of problems is a giant step toward a longer life.
- Know your cholesterol level (it ought to be below 200); and the ratio of your good cholesterol (HDL) to total cholesterol (TC). Divide TC by HDL. A number 4.5 or lower is good.
- Get regular dental checkups and cleaning. The saying, "An ounce of prevention is worth a pound of cure," is more than true for dental and medical issues.

Safety.—This is safety on your behalf as well as on behalf of others.
- Learn CPR. You only have to use it once to make it worthwhile.
- Learn basic first aid. Again, used once, always appreciated. Get a first-aid kit.
- Use your seat belt, and have others who ride with you use them—even those in the back seat.

Your choice.—It is all a matter of choices. The National Wellness Institute emphasizes this by saying your quality of life is impacted:
- 53 percent by the choices you make over the course of your lifetime.
- 21 percent by your environment and surroundings.
- 16 percent by your hereditary factors.
- 10 percent by the medical system.

All these factors are significant. You can easily tell the one that has the most impact. What you choose to eat, your activity level, and your medical and safety practices impact your quality of life. Quality of life relates to your choices over a lifetime—not just for a season.

By Tommy Yessick, Minister's Wellness, Recreation and Sports Ministry Specialist, Ministry Team Leadership Department, LifeWay Church Resources, Nashville, Tennessee.

38. (HOW TO) Ensure Your Social Well-being

Social well-being is effective interaction with others. It includes nurturing current relationships while developing satisfying new ones. This does not mean you are best friends with everyone. Making friends and developing relationships is easier for some people than for others. Good social well-being includes an interdependence with family, a mutual respect with friends, satisfying interaction with acquaintances, and a degree of community involvement.

Family.—When the sun sets on your ministry, your greatest legacy will be your family. Consider the following:
- A survey of 1,400 pastors indicated that half were out of the house half the nights after dinner.
- According to 1,000 spouses of ministers, a major source of stress is finding time as a couple.
- Now add the perception that one third of ministers believe "the ministry" is hazardous to their family.

Get the picture? What are you doing about it? After all, God created the family before He gave us the church. Your greatest investment may be in times of joy, laughter, tears, celebration, and even conflict resolution. Ask yourself these questions, "Is the way I relate to my family, in light of my ministry, a valid model for my child(ren) if they choose to go into ministry? Would my example lead my child not to become a minister, even if God called?"

Consider doing the following in the name of family:
- Plan a regular date with your spouse. If your evening schedule is too crowded, considering meeting her for lunch. She has to eat, even if she works outside the home.
- Give her a whole day occasionally. Arrange your schedule, appointments, details (i.e., children) so the two of you can spend a leisurely paced day together. Do some things she enjoys, some you enjoy, and some you both enjoy.
- Give your kids some real time. It is their time. Let them plan what you will do. Take walks. Go to a park. Go get ice cream. (Whenever you do this, be sure to bring your mind with you and not leave it on work.)

Friends.—Those intimate associates you can count on. Most people have three to five friends they connect with over their lifetime and who unconditionally accept them anytime—no matter what goes wrong, no matter what you need to talk about. It doesn't even matter how long it has been since your last conversation. You can really experience quality conversation. The time together, whether a long-distance phone call or face-to-face conversation, is honest and worthwhile.

Try this. Call someone you have not communicated with in a month or more. Think of a person with whom you were once good friends. Maybe this was in college or seminary. Maybe they were from a previous church. Call them.

Call your spouse. Right now. Just call. After all, she ought to be one of these friends who accepts you.

Ask God to bring you new close friends.

Community.—You live there. Get involved there. Yes, you are the pastor; and by virtue of your role, you are involved in the community. But get involved as a person who lives there. Coach a ball team. Play on a ball team. Help at the school. Volunteer as part of a community project.

The idea is to become involved with people in a much less formal situation than anything related to church. Doing this will help you maintain a perspective for the area in which you live and minister, and it will allow others to experience you as a real person, not just a pastor.

The threefold strand of a cord cannot be broken.

By Tommy Yessick, Minister's Wellness, Recreation and Sports Ministry Specialist, Ministry Team Leadership Department, LifeWay Church Resources, Nashville, Tennessee.

39. (HOW TO) Keep Fresh Yo Well-being

This may be easier said than done for you, the minister. Just because you are about the Lord's work does not automatically mean you are going to keep a spiritual freshness. And the solution is not as easy as the deodorant commercial where a brand swap will keep you fresh all day. You can't just swap a few Scripture verses to heighten your spiritual freshness. Consider and work on the following as you reach for spiritual well-being.

Spiritual Bankruptcy

Bankruptcy is a case where bills and debt greatly exceed your true ability to pay. It is being so far behind with absolutely no way of catching up. It may even include someone else taking over control of your income. It may mean a drastic change in lifestyle. Synonymous terms include financial failure, insolvency, defaulting, economic death, or financial disaster. Can the same happen spiritually? Yes!

You can find yourself in a state of spiritual insolvency. It happens. Here are some ways to avoid finding yourself spiritually overdrawn.

Personal Devotion

Devotion is not the same as preparation for a ministerial duty, like preaching or teaching. This is preparation for you. A few moments with God make your spirit ready for the battles of the day. It is a regular time of listening to God through Scripture and prayer. Out of your spiritual reserve from personal devotion you will find the resources to minister because time alone with God builds your spirit to be more like Jesus.

Your quiet time with God will help you maintain perspective in all the demands of life. You will find God's place in all that you do. It is a great stress buffer as it tends to set a realistic view of what is going in your life. It will also help you to remember that there is no panic in heaven.

Rest

You need two types of rest—physical and emotional. Both feed your spiritual well-being. Physically, to be your spiritual best you must have adequate rest. Sleep allows your body time to rebuild and refresh. Research indicates about seven to seven and one-half hours sleep is optimal to maintain your physical integrity.

The other type of rest is time away. Mark 6:31 tells of Jesus' admonition to come away for a time of rest. Make time to get away. Daniel Spaite, M.D. says the real ticking time bomb in the church is an explosive ministerial burnout. It is not a cultural, denominational, or theological issue but the person of the minister crashing.

Time away from the "press of the crowd" will defuse this time bomb. Move away from a schedule of sick calls, funerals, sermon preparation, counseling, and committee meetings to a time of spiritual and emotional rest. You may find two hours during the week, one day away per month, and three to five days sometime during the year to listen to God, to reflect, and to anticipate your tomorrows. Every five to seven years, you may want to schedule an extended time of one to four months. The seven-year sabbatical is a biblical concept anyway, isn't it? A minister constantly surrounded by others cannot continue to minister to others.

Accountability

This may be difficult. Strongly consider being accountable to someone. Developing accountability relationships will build you up, encourage you, and nurture your spiritual well-being. Find two or three men who will help you, and you them. Through prayer and counsel, decide areas of your life in which you want to be held accountable. Together you help each other develop spiritual well-being and ultimately total well-being. You may choose to be accountable in such ways as time with spouse, time with children, personal devotion, or exercise. Together you pray, seek God's answer, and decide to move.

Your spiritual well-being impacts your social, mental, and physical well-being. When you are at your best spiritually, you feel better physically and mentally, and you relate better to others when your spiritual bank account has a surplus.

By Tommy Yessick, Minister's Wellness, Recreation and Sports Ministry Specialist, Ministry Team Leadership Department, LifeWay Church Resources, Nashville, Tennessee.

40. (HOW TO) Stay on Top of Your Vocational Well-being

One of the best pieces of advice for your vocational well-being is to realize this quote from a fellow pastor: "I have come to realize that I can't do everything. I am part of God's plan; I am not God's plan."

Staying fresh in ministry is no easy task. Some of the following will help you.

Describe your call.—Recount your call to ministry. Write out your call to the ministry. It doesn't have to be long or eloquent, but write it down. Then write out your call to your present place of ministry. How did you come to know it was the right place to be? Both of these will help you refresh your call.

What are you trying to do?—*Vision statement* is what some call it. It may be called a mission statement. Either way you ought to be able to express, either in writing or verbally, your vision or mission statement. If you cannot do this, take time to think about it and to develop one. Such a statement will help you immensely.

It will help you make decisions and choices. Do you ever get caught asking yourself: "Should I do *A* or *B*? Should I choose *X* or *Y*?" The fact is *A*, *B*, *X*, and *Y* may all be good. A mission statement will help you decide which of these good choices will help you and your church fulfill its mission.

Accentuate appreciation.—Take time to appreciate your coworkers—other staff members or the two or three key leaders who work with you, if you are a one-person staff. Imagine what you would have to add to your to-do list if those people where not around to assist you. Take a moment to list a few things they do for the church and the kingdom of God. Now tell them of your appreciation for their contribution to the ministry in your area.

If you have trouble doing this, try finding out more about what they do. You will increase your appreciation as you discover all that these other leaders do for the kingdom.

Expressing appreciation for others will help you. Others' appreciation for you will also increase.

Keep learning.–Learn something new. Read a book or article. Take a class related to some area of your work. The time invested to do this will pay dividends.

Attend a seminar or conference sponsored by an evangelical organization. These are offered on national, regional, state, and local levels.

Take a class not related to your work–maybe a new hobby. Consider a class offered at a home-improvement store.

Manage your money.–How does this relate to vocational well-being? Through your vocation you earn your money. It is probably less than you would like, but you are called to be a steward, a manager of what you are "given." Besides, managed money goes farther.

Do this by spending every incoming dollar before the month begins. Begin with the basics–giving, savings (even if it is a small amount), housing, food, transportation. Then allocate for categories that are absolutely necessary. The idea is to give every dollar a name. Agree on this with your spouse. Then follow the plan. If mid-month changes need to be made, and they will, pray and discuss the changes with your spouse. Put money most often used for cash purchases such as food, gas, or clothes in envelopes. This leads to the next part of managing money, pay cash.

Do away with credit cards. Research indicates you do not spend as much when you pay cash as when you use credit cards. "The borrower is servant to the lender" (Prov. 22:7). You are not to be servant to anyone except God.

To summarize, these steps will help you find and keep balance in your vocation:
- Write out your call to ministry.
- Write out your call to your current place of service.
- Write out your vision/mission statement.
- Express appreciation for coworkers and key leaders.
- Learn something new.
- Manage your money by getting rid of credit cards and planning your next month's spending.

By Tommy Yessick, Minister's Wellness, Recreation and Sports Ministry Specialist, Ministry Team Leadership Department, LifeWay Church Resources, Nashville, Tennessee.

41. (HOW TO) Manage Stress: Be Resilient

Resilience is the strong ability to cope during times of depravation, adversity, or stress. Resilience is the ability to get through the high stress periods of change and come out on the other side with a strong sense of well-being.

Before you get to the point of tying a knot at the end of your rope, identify and work on the following characteristics of resilience.

Independence of thought and action, without fear or reluctance to rely on others.—When you are doing right in God's eyes—not your own or others', you should have an independence surpassing all else. In 2 Timothy 1:7, note that God does not give a spirit of fear.

The ability to give and take in one's interaction with others.—You live in a world with others. You work with others. Look at the model of Jesus. He was around people in many informal situations.

A network of friends, including one or more confidants.—These need not be many. A few good friends can mean much to your stress level. Just knowing they are there to talk with you, to discuss your difficulties, may provide just the support you need.

A high level of personal discipline and sense of responsibility.—Commit yourself to read the Bible every day. Read in the Psalms. Read Romans. Read and reread Scriptures of encouragement, for example Psalm 37 and Jeremiah 29, especially verse 11.

Recognition and development of special gifts and talents.—Reidentify one of your spiritual gifts. Write down how that gift helps your present place of ministry. What would happen if you developed that gift more fully?

A willingness to dream.—Slow down long enough to dream. Look out the window. Go for a walk and imagine new ways. Dream of something that has absolutely nothing to do with a current program or ministry where you serve.

A wide range of interests.—The sheer accomplishment of even a small task helps boost your spirits. So whether it's gardening, fishing, collecting, woodworking, hiking, drawing, sketching, or any other type of hobby, take time to enjoy it. It will be good for you and others.

Insight into one's own feelings and those of others and the ability to communicate feelings appropriately.—Learn to deal with four general emotions. "To deal with" does not mean to hide or suppress, rather learn to express these emotions appropriately. The emotions are glad, sad, mad, and scared. (See 35. "How to Nurture Emotional Well-being" for more on these four emotions.)

Focus, a commitment to life, and a philosophical framework.—Maintaining your focus within personal experiences can help you interpret life with meaning and hope, even at life's seemingly hopeless moments. As a minister, what is your commitment to life? What is the philosophy from which you work? If you grasp, really know, your own commitment and philosophy, you will be steps ahead when you must make difficult decisions. Maintaining your focus will help you through times when hope is distant.

Take time to write down your commitment. Complete each of the following in the order presented:

1. My commitment to God is _____

_____

_____

2. My commitment to my family is _____

_____

_____

3. My commitment to my work is _____

_____

_____

By Tommy Yessick, Minister's Wellness, Recreation and Sports Ministry Specialist, Ministry Team Leadership Department, LifeWay Church Resources, Nashville, Tennessee.

42. (HOW TO) Manage Stress: Be Hardy

Hardiness means you are less likely to be affected by the external things which impact your daily life.

Perception.—"As a man thinketh, so is he." Perception can be the filter for all your decisions, attitudes, and actions. Reality and perception often are not the same. A gap exists between what is real and what you perceive.

Check the reality of your perception. Next time you face a stressful situation, answer the following questions. As you answer them, consider yourself, your family, and your ministry in the short- and long-term.

1. What is the immediate value or consequence of the situation? Write down a few of the immediate results of the problem. Include both the good and bad sides.
2. What will be the consequences of the same situation tomorrow? If left unchanged, what would happen tomorrow?
3. What will be the value of a decision next week?
4. What will be the value in one year?
5. What will be the value five years from now?

Taking time to answer these five questions will provide a more accurate perception.

Commitment versus alienation.—Commitment is the framework which helps you through difficulties. It causes you to be actively involved in life—work, family, and social life. It is a strong belief that what you do has meaning and purpose. Commitment helps prevent you from being hindered by fear.

The alienated person is driven by fear and the external. Though tangible results are often helpful, commitment can sustain as a long-term source of energy. Alienation causes one to be removed, detached, and somewhat isolated while just watching the world go by. These people are content with the status quo.

Commitment allows you to take risks and become energized by your deep desire to be what God wants you to be in all areas of your life.

Control versus helplessness.—Control is the sense of making a difference. You can make an impact where you minister. People with this trait don't wait for bad things to happen, then try to correct them. They anticipate change and plan for ways to take advantage of that change, as opposed to feeling unable to do anything, which is helplessness.

Helplessness, the opposite of this type control, is the idea that no matter what happens, no matter what you do, you cannot make a difference. It is a view of being useless and that nothing matters.

Challenge versus threat.—Challenge requires a certain amount of vigor as you approach changes with a sense of excitement. Seeing possibilities instead of pitfalls is the challenge approach to what life and work bring to your path. This is not just a quick, superficial attitude. It is a way of thinking, approaching, and viewing all that comes your way. It is fueled by gaining a sense of growth, mastery, and accomplishment from solving the "puzzles" that are always there.

On the other hand, seeing life's problems as threats holds back the work of the kingdom. How? If you are afraid something is not going to work, that an idea will not be accepted, or that a program might not be exactly perfect, you'll never get anywhere. Threat paralyzes you from moving, even the least bit, in the right direction.

"I will instruct and teach you in the way which you should go" (Ps. 32:8, NASB).

"'I know the plans that I have for you,' says the Lord, 'plans for welfare not for calamity, to give you a future and a hope'" (Jer. 29:11, NASB).

By Tommy Yessick, Minister's Wellness, Recreation and Sports Ministry Specialist, Ministry Team Leadership Department, LifeWay Church Resources, Nashville, Tennessee.

43. (HOW TO) Manage Stress: Verify Values

One of the great inducers of stress is you. Well, maybe not you but the way you approach valuable aspects of your life, the way you approach the tasks of the day. The way you deal with what is important can create anxiety.

Often you build up stress in a kind of subconscious way. It sneaks up on you. You begin to notice uneasiness building. Things just don't seem to be right. The stress builds, and you are not sure why. Or it may more blatant as stress meets you head-on.

Stress can be traced to the difference between what you believe is important and what requires most of your energy. Do this little exercise to see.

What is important to you? Write down what is important. Think of the many different things which are important. These may relate to people, places, or things.

_____

_____

_____

_____

_____

_____

_____

_____

_____

Review the items and assign each of the items you've listed either 1, 2, or 3, based on importance with 1 being absolutely important, 2 being important but you can choose to do without, and 3 is not really necessary, you just like to have it around.

Review again your list and rating. Are there themes for the *1*s, for the *2*s, and for the *3*s?

See how closely your list of important things fall into these areas—health, home, and work.

Most of the things you listed probably relate to either your health—such as sleeping, eating, or maybe even exercise, relationships, lifestyle habits; home—including spouse, family, extended family; and work—people, coworkers, church sermon preparation, teaching work.

You create tension when you deal with your areas of importance—health, home, work, or anything else. The stress comes, and for that matter intensifies, when your energy and what you value are not in sync. Notice the word is *energy*, not *time*. You may have something that is important, but you do not put as much time in it as you do something else. For instance, family may be a high value (and well it should). However, you put more time into your work. The question is beyond time; it is energy.

A better approach may be this. How hard do you try to spend time with your family? Do you really make it a must to talk with your children. If you have no children living at home, what effort do you put forth to talk to your spouse. Now "talking to them" does not mean talking "at" them or talking, as in correcting and disciplining. It is instead the degree of commitment you make to set aside time and follow through on that time.

Another way to think of this is, When you go home from work, are you able to take your mind with you? Can you give your attention to your family? If you take a vacation, how long does it take to relax and enjoy yourself? Or are you still "working"? Do you allow yourself time to work on your health? If not, you are going to undermine the length and effectiveness of your ministry and life.

Commit time and energy to home, health, and work for a long, productive tenure of service to the kingdom of God.

If you could measure your energy to your commitments and you find a match between that and what you value, you would find a corresponding reduction in stress.

By Tommy Yessick, Minister's Wellness, Recreation and Sports Ministry Specialist, Ministry Team Leadership Department, LifeWay Church Resources, Nashville, Tennessee.

94

44. **HOW TO** Keep It All Together– Total Well-being

Integration is beneficial to understanding total well-being. What happens in one area of your life has ramifications in other areas. Just as you do not function in a vacuum in your everyday life, no dimension of you operates in a void. The way you feel physically (e.g, you've got the flu) impacts the way you function mentally. The way you feel emotionally (e.g, stressed out) can influence the way you function physically, socially (relate to family), even spiritually.

The more you understand the integration and interrelationship of all parts of your life, the more you will see how nurturing one area can help the others. Also you can understand the importance of devoting some energy to every aspect of your life–emotional, intellectual, physical, social, spiritual, and vocational.

Spiritual well-being impacts. . . .
- *Social well-being.*–Values and beliefs become evident in social situations.
- *Vocational well-being.*–Call to ministry and to current service according to God's purpose for your life. Work is best when your talents, gifts, and desire come into concert with God's will for you.
- *Physical well-being.*–Appreciation for God's creation helps clarify a strong relationship between body, mind, and spirit. Motivates self-care.
- *Intellectual well-being.*–Aids understanding one's place in God's creation.
- *Emotional well-being.*–Promotes a realistic view of stressors. Allows time for reflection and introspection.

Physical well-being impacts. . . .
- *Social well-being.*–Increased stamina and improved appearance enhance acceptance and provide a better role model for others.
- *Vocational well-being.*–Improves performance and ability to survive difficult situations.
- *Spiritual well-being.*–Enhances the relationship between sound body and sound mind.
- *Emotional well-being.*–Improves self-control and self-discipline. Serves as a coping mechanism for stress.

Social well-being impacts. . . .
- *Vocational well-being.*–Interpersonal skills promote cooperation, satisfaction, and growth among coworkers and members.

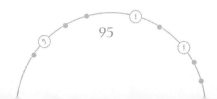

95

- *Spiritual well-being.*—Communication with others nurtures Christian fellowship, while developing, and deepening personal convictions.
- *Physical well-being.*—Family and friends support health, fitness, and nutrition and provide comfort in times of illness.
- *Intellectual well-being.*—Others can encourage opportunities to learn.
- *Emotional well-being.*—Friends and family offer support.

Emotional well-being impacts. . . .
- *Social well-being.*—Provides patience for others in all situations.
- *Vocational well-being.*—Allows better temperament for job-related challenges. Lessens the impact of short-term, stressful job situations.
- *Spiritual well-being.*—Allows for healthier self-reflection and evaluation.
- *Physical well-being.*—Reduces risk of disease and assists in healing.
- *Intellectual well-being.*—Encourages problem solving.

Intellectual well-being impacts. . . .
- *Social well-being.*—Supports interaction, acceptance, and understanding.
- *Vocational well-being.*—Increases support for greater work challenges.
- *Spiritual well-being.*—Encourages thorough investigation of beliefs.
- *Physical well-being.*—Supports understanding of the body, the importance of its care, and how to improve physical well-being.
- *Emotional well-being.*—More easily recognizes emotionally trying situations and formulates appropriate responses.

Vocational well-being impacts. . . .
- *Social well-being.*—Call to ministry and to current location helps provide acceptance, understanding, and teamwork.
- *Spiritual well-being.*—Reassures the sense of call to ministry, current position, present location of service.
- *Physical well-being.*—Reduced job stress improves physical health.
- *Intellectual well-being.*—Provides fresh opportunities to grow and expand your knowledge base.
- *Emotional well-being.*—Satisfaction in ministry and work supports sound emotional health.

To stay on top of your total well-being, review the other wellness articles in this section of this book.

By Tommy Yessick, Minister's Wellness, Recreation and Sports Ministry Specialist, Ministry Team Leadership Department, LifeWay Church Resources, Nashville, Tennessee.

Resource

Yessick, Tommy. *Building Blocks for Longer Life and Ministry.* Nashville: Convention Press, 1997.

45. (HOW TO) Feed Your Body: The Truth on Nutrition

Good nutrition helps maintain and build structural integrity within the body. Nutrition is consuming the 45 essential nutrients, digesting and absorbing these nutrients, transporting the nutrients to the cell, metabolizing these nutrients, and eliminating the waste, while maintaining proper weight.

Your body works best when you get the proper amount of all of these nutrients. Your body requires more than 100,000 chemicals to perform all the different functions necessary to sustain a strong, healthy life. While your body contains or can produce many of the necessary building blocks for these chemicals, some must come from an outside source–food.

Carbohydrates

Function.–Carbohydrates provide energy, energy storage (short- and long-term), vitamin and mineral source.

Sources.–Fruits, vegetables, whole-grain products, pasta, legumes.

Need.–Carbohydrates should supply 55–65 percent of your calories. This is your body's best source of energy. Complex carbohydrates are the desired source. What are these?

Fruits and vegetables.–Eat two to four servings of each. They are great sources of fiber, vitamins, and minerals, as well as chemicals, which may have a buffer against heart disease and cancer.

Fresh is best. Eat raw fruits and vegetables when possible. Generally fresh should be followed by frozen, then canned.

Grains.–Whole-grain products supply fiber and nutrients. Sources include brown rice, whole-wheat breads, whole-grain cereals.

Legumes.–These are great sources of fiber, protein, vitamins, and minerals.

Potatoes and other starchy vegetables.–Many people avoid potatoes because they consider them fattening. Potatoes are fattening when you add butter, sour cream, and bacon bits!

Dietary Fats (lipids)

Function.–This fuel source provides and carries essential nutrients (Vitamins A, D, E, K, and linoleic acid), provides for certain body structure, protects and insulates, and provides food satiety.

Sources.–Dairy products, meats, fish, poultry, eggs, oils, nuts, seeds, and many snack foods such as potato and corn chips.

Need.–Dietary fats can supply up to 20–30 percent of your calories.
Tips on fats.
• Bake or broil fish and chicken.
• Use corn, safflower, or canola oil for cooking.
• Drink and cook with 1 percent (low-fat) or skim (no-fat) milk.
• Select leaner cuts of beef.

Protein

Function.–Protein provides structure and regulates body processes through enzymes and hormones.

Sources.–Animal sources include meat, fish, poultry, eggs, and milk. Plant sources include green vegetables and legumes.

Need.–Protein should supply 12–15 percent of your caloric intake–about 3 ounces of beef or chicken per day.

Vitamins

Fat-soluble (A, D, E, K) and water-soluble (the B vitamins and C) vitamins are organic compounds necessary for metabolic reactions within your body. While vitamins provide no actual energy, they facilitate the energy-releasing reactions that promote your body's growth, development, and maintenance.

Minerals

Your body needs 19 essential minerals. These are generally supplied through a balanced diet consisting of a mix of animal and vegetable products. Major minerals, requiring more than 100 mg. a day are calcium, phosphorus, magnesium, sodium, chloride, potassium, and sulfur. Trace minerals have a daily nutritional need of less than 100 mg. These are iron, zinc, selenium, iodine, copper, fluoride, molybdenum, chromium, and manganese.

Water

Water is absolutely necessary for the efficient completion of every chemical process in your body. Water is a source of minerals, a solvent and transporter of nutrients, a lubricant, a temperature regulator, a growth promoter, a catalyst, and an acid-base balance. You need at least 64 ounces of water per day. Caffeine-laden liquids do not count and even have an opposite effect.

By Tommy Yessick, Minister's Wellness, Recreation and Sports Ministry Specialist, Ministry Team Leadership Department, LifeWay Church Resources, Nashville, Tennessee.

46. (HOW TO) Care for Persons in Crisis

A couple welcomes a new baby into their home; a woman has experienced a painful divorce; an elderly man loses his mate of 50 years; a middle-aged man must change vocations; an unmarried teenage girl is pregnant; and a young family must relocate to a new city. As a minister, you often help individuals during these times. Crisis situations demand our ministry. A crisis is a time of opportunity. What must we do when we recognize a crisis situation? Five suggestions are offered.

Assess the Situation

During crisis situations ask yourself a few questions. What are the needs of the individuals? Are those needs being met? Can I mobilize others to help? What can I do? When should I go? How long should I stay? Is the crisis severe enough to require an immediate response? Is the crisis something I need to respond to at all? After making an assessment, you will be able to respond in a wise and reasoned manner.

Be Available

Your availability should be threefold—before, during, and after the crisis. Before the crisis you earn the right to minister. You prove you care. During the crisis you put your faith into action. After the crisis the need may be greatest because other support has moved on.

Accept the Person

Pastors are likely to encounter those contemplating suicide, homosexuals, unwed mothers, murderers, thieves, those impacted by a dread disease, divorcees, and many other crisis situations. An understanding, accepting attitude will enhance your ability to minister to such individuals.

This idea of acceptance is amply illustrated in Job's three friends: Eliphaz, Bildad, and Zophar. When they first visited Job, they were content to sit quietly; however, they could not resist the temptation to give advice. These friends told Job everything that was wrong without stopping to understand or listen to him. They could not accept Job and his questions.

Give Assurance

You may give assurance in several ways. Read a carefully selected passage of
Scripture. Give assurance by leaving a comforting pamphlet or booklet.
Give assurance by the gentle touch of a hand. Give assurance through being
silent. For some reason most people feel they always must say something to
people experiencing crisis. Sometimes the best comfort is to say nothing.

Give Assistance

Ministers usually know about service agencies that help people during times
of crisis, such as the Red Cross, funeral homes, counseling centers, govern-
ment services, and volunteer services. Sharing information or locating
information is greatly needed service during a crisis. Timely information
could ease a state of panic. Consider building a file that contains the names
of helping agencies.

Another way ministers can offer assistance is in the area of decision
making. People experiencing crisis often are confused and display distorted
decision-making capability. You can help them explore alternatives and offer
clearheaded suggestions that may have been overlooked.

No single formula is right for every crisis. Ministering during crises is
difficult. No one can state with authority what must be done during these
times. Ministers always should be learning, growing, and developing in
caring ministries.

Adapted from Tim Patrick, "Caring for Persons in Times of Crisis," *Church Administration*, March
1989, 23–24.

Resource

Caregiving. A quarterly newsletter published by LifeWay Church Resources.
    For more information or to order call 1-800-458-2772.

47. (HOW TO) Minister to People Who Are Grieving

The death of a loved one is not the only reason people grieve. The death of a meaningful relationship can also cause significant grief. Sometimes a treasured relationship is lost because of a misunderstanding. A grieving person may find himself pretending it didn't happen, experiencing anger because it happened, and then becoming depressed.

Persons also grieve when their marriage is dissolved through divorce. In this imperfect world the biblical ideal of marriage (one man and one woman for a lifetime) fails. I've know churches that grieved when they lost a pastor that most folks were glad to see go! People grieve the loss of imperfect relationships.

People grieve the loss of dreams. A person puts his or her whole life into starting a business only to have it fail. Grief is sure to follow. Parents have high hopes for a child only to see that child destroyed through some action.

The Stages of Grief

Grief is not predictable. Each person grieves in his own way. Persons who have studied grief do see some common elements to grieving. Granger Westberg, in his classic *Good Grief*, listed 10 stages of grieving:

Stage 1.—We are in a state of shock/denial. "It can't be."

Stage 2.—We express emotion/release (tears).

Stage 3.—We feel depressed and lonely. "No one understands."

Stage 4.—We may experience physical symptoms of distress. "I can't go on."

Stage 5.—We may become panicky. "I can't make it."

Stage 6.—We feel a sense of guilt about the loss. "If only I. . . ." or, "Why didn't I?"

Stage 7.–We are filled with hostility and resentment. "Why me?"

Stage 8.–We are unable to return to usual activities. "I don't want to go out."

Stage 9.–Gradually hope comes through. "Someday–maybe."

Stage 10.–We struggle to readjust to reality. "I'll get on with it."[1]

Grievers do not move through these stages in a linear fashion. That is, they do not finish stage 1 and progress to stage 2. Rather, they may be in shock/denial in this moment, but one hour later they're in stage 10, adjusting to the reality of life. Grievers bounce back and forth through the various stages of grief.

Three Practical Questions

How long does grief take to finish its course?–Getting over grief can take as long as one to three years. Often in ministry to grieving persons, pastors try to rush the grief process along (probably out of their own discomfort).

What should you say to someone who has sustained a significant loss?–The best answer is, very little. Your presence (both physically and emotionally) is far more likely to be remembered than what you say.

How can you minister to grieving persons?
1. Admit to yourself that you are a griever. Look honestly at what scares you about grief.
2. Be more willing to listen to the griever than to tell him what he ought to do.
3. Be concrete in your ministry to persons in the throes of grief.
4. Be willing to back off and let your relationship with the grieving person return to normal as she adjusts to her loss.

---

[1]Granger Westberg, *Good Grief* (Philadelphia: Fortress Press, 1971).

48. (HOW TO) Improve Your Listening Skills

Pastors spend a lot of time listening—at least they should. The honest fact is that some pastors find listening difficult. I can understand. Pastors stand up on Sunday and look in the faces of a congregation of people who look to them for a word from God. Speaking is an important part of the ministry—and not just speaking but preaching, preaching a message that tells the congregation what God would say to them this week from His Word.

Even though communicating through preaching is important, don't forget about the importance of listening. Those same people who look to you for a word from God need to know you are listening to them. Listening takes time. It requires that you be genuinely interested. It insists that you have a real servant spirit.

I have had the privilege of hearing some of the greatest pastors and preachers of our day. It may surprise you to know that almost to a man I found them to be good listeners in a one-on-one situation.

In *Called to Care*, compiled by Jim Hightower, I found some tips on listening that have been helpful to me.

1. Carefully attend.
   - Attend to physical and emotional behavior.
   - Face them—eye contact.
   - Consider seating arrangements.
   - Use an open posture—not crossed arms or legs.
   - Minimize distractions and interruptions.
2. Respond empathetically.
3. Ask clarifying and open-ended questions.
   - Use few questions.
   - Use questions which clarify and generate further self-exploration.
4. Risk self-disclosure.
   - Do not shift to your story.
   - Reveal your thoughts and feelings which result from what you have heard.
5. Challenge and confront appropriately; point out what you see.
   - Distortions.
   - Self-delusions
   - Blind spots.

6. Be careful. Don't use confrontation to communicate anger, impatience, or disgust.[1]

Helpful Hints

Ask questions.—Avoid questions that can be answered with yes or no. Try to ask questions that explore feelings. For example, ask, "How did you feel when that happened?" rather than, "Did that make you angry?"

Avoid interrogation.—Let people explore their issues in their own time. Do not try to rush them or to satisfy your own curiosity.

Don't pretend to listen in order to talk.—Sometimes a person who pretends to be listening is merely marking time until the person talking takes a breath and the talking-listening process is reversed. Focus on what the person is saying.

Listen with empathy.—Try to understand the other person's situation. Show sincerity. Face reality. Trust the Holy Spirit to work in a person's life without your preaching. Follow Christ's example.

Adapted from Donna J. Gandy, Ruth L. Hendrix, James E. Hightower Jr., *Improving Your Listening Skills: Ministering in Times of Crisis* (Nashville: Convention Press, 1993), 9–12.

[1]Steve Ivy, "Helping by Hearing, Understanding, and Relating to Feelings," *Called to Care*, James E. Hightower, Jr., compiler (Nashville: Convention Press, 1990), 82-84.

49. (HOW TO) Begin a Special Education Ministry in Your Church

People and families with special needs often long for ministry. Special education programs in our schools are full. Most group homes for special needs adults have waiting lists. People with physical disabilities are everywhere. Millions of people in the United States have special needs.

Learn about people with special needs.—The leader of a special needs Sunday School class spoke to the mother of one of her class members. "Tell me about your son," asked the Sunday School teacher, "What are his interests? I would really like to get to know him."

The mother replied, "My son is 30 years old, and this is the first time anyone has shown this kind of interest in him."

Discover needs in your community.—Get to know people who work with those you want to reach.
• Schoolteachers
• Occupational and physical therapists
• Neurologists
• Sheltered workshop personnel
• Group home managers
Even though agencies will not usually provide you with a list of names and addresses, they may cooperate in many other ways. An effective picture brochure or flyer may be distributed or perhaps even sent home with each person.

Prepare your church for this type ministry.—Suppose a person with a significant physical disability decided to come to your church this Sunday. Would a suitable parking place be available? Does every building have at least one primary entrance which would be suitable for individuals in wheelchairs? Are suitable rest room facilities available?

While you may not be able to eliminate every inappropriate stare, it should be possible to prepare your congregation for the arrival of people with special needs. If you have the opportunity, talk with the congregation about the possibility that people with special needs may be coming to your church. Remind them to be friendly, and treat these people with dignity.

Determine the ministry you should begin.—Opportunities to minister to persons with special needs are unlimited. All that is needed to begin is a love for people, a genuine interest in people with special needs, and a willingness to learn. Here are a few ideas to get you started.

Homebound ministries.—Caring for persons with special needs can be a 24-hour-a-day task. Perhaps your ministry could include providing respite time for caregivers.

Special needs Sunday School class.—Workers who are willing to learn and be trained can provide a meaningful Bible study experience for persons with special needs. Excellent Bible study resources and training materials are available from LifeWay Christian Resources. For more information call 1-800-458-2772.

Existing Sunday School classes.—Determining which approach is best may be difficult. Should the church start a special needs class or involve special needs people in the existing organization?

To answer this question two factors must be considered.

1. Can the needs of the special-needs person be met in the existing class? Everyone should have the opportunity to learn at his or her own level. Perhaps a helper could be enlisted for the special needs person and some modifications made which would make this possible.
2. Can the needs of others in the existing class be met while ministering to special needs members? Sometimes the condition of a special needs person may make it impossible for them to be included in existing classes and still allow workers to minister to others in the group.

Ministry to children with special needs.—The child with Attention Deficit Hyperactivity Disorder (ADHD) could benefit greatly from some individual attention. A helper could be enlisted to assist this child during Sunday School.

Resource

McNay, Athalene. *A Place for Everyone: A Guide for Special Education Bible Teaching-Reaching Ministry.* Nashville: Convention Press, 1997.

50. HOW TO Help a Hurting Pastor

What are some helpful things you can do to ease the pain of a fellow pastor who either is in conflict within himself or within his church? Here is some practical advice.

Make a Personal Visit to the Home of the Hurting Pastor

A phone call is good, but it does not fulfill your pastor-friend's needs– someone to talk to face-to-face, someone who sincerely wants to ease the pain. When you phone the pastor, the conversation usually is begun with the question, How are you doing? A pastor who is hurting will hesitate to share his true feelings on the phone because he has no eye contact with you. Eye contact gives you the opportunity to share with the hurting pastor that you really do care how he is doing and that you are not just being ministerially inquisitive.

Write an Understanding Letter

Letters can have an amazing, healing effect on one who is hurting. They serve two important purposes in the healing process. When one receives a letter of compassion from a friend, he has the opportunity to read it several times. He might not remember what you verbally say, but he can keep available for his reference what you write. Second, not only does the friend get to read your letter, but he has the opportunity to share it with another person. That might be crucial for his own personal self-image.

Letters also serve to minister to one's spouse. Sometimes the spouse is inaccessible. In such times a letter allows you to say those words of comfort and encouragement.

Perform a Tangible Deed of Love

A sensitive pastor/friend can do several things to help ease the hurt of another pastor. Probably the first thing to do is to ask yourself, "What would be most helpful to me if I were in his shoes?" By answering that question, you can better understand the needs of a person who is abruptly terminated from a ministerial position. Let me propose a few things for your consideration:

107

- Show up some day or evening with the offer (or make advance arrangements) to take the children out for an activity to allow the hurting couple to have some precious time alone.
- Show up some day or evening to take the minister out for coffee or just for a drive to give him an opportunity to share his feelings. This also will give him time to get away from the situation. Your wife could do the same for the wife of the minister.
- Money, food, and housing needs may soon be critical. Your awareness of this fact will allow you to know that talking about these needs will be most difficult for the terminated pastor as well as for you. You will have many opportunities to minister through love offerings, poundings, and providing shelter for the family.
- Pray for the pastor's situation, and encourage other like-minded pastors to pray also. Be sure to let the pastor know you are praying for him.

No one solution will meet every need. Every hurting pastor and family is different, thus the healing will be different. Your sensitivity to his heartbreak and to his feelings of failure will do more to allow you to minister to his needs than anything else. Remember, everyone needs a hand to hold onto at some time. May you be that hand of support for someone today.

51. (HOW TO) Minister to People Who Have Lost a Loved One to Death

In a recent presentation a pastor described how he and his family were sheltered in the arms of God during the loss of their teenage granddaughter. During this time of incredible personal loss and grief, my friend learned some important lessons about ministering to others in times of grief. I asked him to write down a few of the lessons he learned during this pilgrimage. The following is adapted from his notes, and I added a few ideas of my own.

Be there with the family.—Your personal presence is important. If a family ever needs their pastor, they need him now. A phone call isn't sufficient. Unless you are in a very large church, no staff member can represent you in this circumstance. Spend time with the grieving family.

Offer to help with necessary funeral arrangements.—You are a professional. This family may have no idea how to plan a service. They may need your help in relating to the funeral home.

Don't use trite religious statements.—Scripture is comforting. The Holy Spirit can comfort in ways we don't even understand. But trite statements about how we should really be happy because our loved one is with the Lord are inappropriate. The Scripture is true. If the one who has died was a believer, he or she is in heaven and with the Lord. This truth, however, does not remove the genuine pain of missing a loved one we won't see again until we die or the Lord returns. To suggest that Christians should not grieve is inappropriate and unscriptural (see 1 Thes. 4:13). We sorrow, but not as those who have no hope.

Hug a lot.—Human touch is therapeutic. It shows your concern and sensitivity. Be sure your hug is appropriate, and express your genuine concern. In some instances an appropriate hand on the shoulder or a warm handshake is best.

Allow people to grieve in their own way.—Some people are quiet; others are expressive. Don't try to analyze, just love them and be there for them.

Some people need to cry. Let them. Others need to talk. Listen. Some just need someone to sit with them in silence.

Be prepared to be silent.—You may not need to say very much. You should pray with them and be ready to share appropriate and comforting Scriptures. But don't feel that your words should make the pain go away. The best ministry may be to sit in silence with them.

Mobilize the church to help in any possible way.—The home may need cleaning or straightening. Child care may help. Food may allow the family freedom from day-to-day tasks such as cooking for the family.

Relate to the family one month after the funeral.—Pastoral ministry may be needed most at this time. All the friends and relatives are gone back home. Life is supposed to have returned to normal. People expect more recovery than is possible. During those quiet, lonely moments, the grieving person may need you.

Send notes of encouragement at six months.—Writing a note will only take you a few moments, but it may be an enormous benefit to a grieving church member.

Be available to listen anytime.—Let the bereaved talk.

Resource

Caregiving. A quarterly newsletter published by LifeWay Church Resources.
    For more information or to order call 1-800-458-2772.

52. (HOW TO) Enlist Volunteer Workers for Your Church

In most churches, enlisting workers (especially Sunday School teachers) is one of the most dreaded tasks. Pastors and nominating committees approach enlistment with the mind-set that people really don't want to do these things and we must talk them into teaching these classes.

I am convinced that your church can find every worker God has for you if you follow these 10 simple steps in enlistment. If you take shortcuts along the way or skip some steps, the guarantee is null and void.

1. Pray.—In Matthew 9:38, Jesus said, "Pray ye therefore the Lord of the harvest, that he will send forth labourers into his harvest." That prayer at the beginning of the nominating committee meeting is nice, but it's not enough. Ask each member of the nominating team to take a portion of the positions to be filled and pray each day for a week. Ask God to show you the one person in the church He would have teach the class. Yes, even pray about the teachers who have been teaching the same class for 20 years. It will be a blessing to go to them and ask them to teach again with confidence that God has confirmed their being in that position.

2. Make a list of needed workers.—Include every position to be filled.

3. Make a list of potential workers.—Include every church member who is capable of serving and acceptable to the church. Many nominating teams say no for people. Someone suggests a person, and another member of the team says: "He won't do it. We asked him last year, and he turned us down." Don't do that! You don't know what God may do in their lives. Your job is to pray and contact the person God leads you to contact.

4. Make a list of training opportunities.—Include the following.
- National training opportunities (Glorieta and Ridgecrest).
- Training offered by your state convention.
- Training offered by your association.
- At least one training event offered at your local church.
- Individual training opportunities designed for self-study.

Include dates and times for each. Don't take a shortcut here! Put these training opportunities on paper.

5. Pray again.—Ask God to lead you to the one person in all the church to teach this class or accept this ministry position.

6. Decide on one person.—Often the nominating committee prays for the leadership of God, decides on a person to contact, and then decides on a backup, just in case the answer is no. Think about that practice. Why do we need a backup? The only reason is we started the process too late, and we don't have time to pray again. Decide on one person. If he or she says no, pray again, "Lord, who is the one person in our church you would have teach this class?"

7. Make an appointment.—This is important. Make a commitment that no one will be enlisted in the hallway or on the parking lot. When we enlist without an appointment, we are saying: "This ministry isn't very important. I didn't even take time to arrange a time and place where we could discuss it." Consider meeting at the church in the room where he or she would teach or minister.

8. Make an enlistment contact.—Tell prospective workers about your prayer and that you feel God has led you to invite them to accept this ministry. Take the teaching materials with you and walk through preparation of a lesson. Don't take a shortcut here! Ask them to pray.

9. Contact potential workers for their reply.—Give them a week to pray. This contact can be made by phone.

10. Follow up.—Invite workers to sit in on a class similar to the one they will be leading. Check with the worker after a month to see how things are going. Make sure those training events really happen.

53. (HOW TO) Motivate Volunteer Workers

The work of the church would be impossible without volunteers. Yet serving as a volunteer in the church can be discouraging at times. What can we, as leaders, do to motivate them?

Effective leaders are motivators. Here are a few tips to help you motivate the volunteer workers in your church.

Guide Leaders to Understand the Mission of the Church

If the church has purpose or vision statements, these will help. In addition, people need to hear the pastor reinforce the mission from the pulpit. They also need to see the mission statement interpreted in print. Plan the ministries and activities of the church in accordance with the mission statement.

- Reinforce a compelling vision for the future.
- Focus on the future rather than the past.

Enlist Workers Who Have a Heart for God and for People

Use a spiritual gifts inventory, and guide workers to grow in their areas of giftedness.

Delegate Responsibility and Expect Accountability

Help workers understand the meaning of their job description. Assist workers in becoming more competent in their work.

Create an Atmosphere in Which Service Is Seen as Valuable and Significant

Sensitize church leaders to the time constraints of volunteers. Generate a feeling of excitement about what God is doing in and through the church fellowship.

Guide Leaders in Their Ability to Accept, Attract, Reach, and Assimilate New People

Continually adding new people will add excitement to your organization. And adding new people will also ensure that new workers are available for training, and then they are available to begin their work and ministry in leadership roles.

Help Volunteers Increase Their Willingness to Accept and Deal Positively with Change

Change happens. Often change is good. Ev en small changes can add engergy to a program. If you listen to your workers, get their input for change, and try to offer options whenever possible, most of the time workers will be more receptive to change.

Keep Volunteers from Taking on Too Much Responsibility

Monitor what leaders are doing. Be sensitive to signs of burnout. Provide enrichment training, renewal opportunities, and encouragement.

Provide Reinforcement and Affirmation Through Meaningful Celebrations

Recognize workers before the people they serve. Recognize leaders on Worker Appreciation Day. Be alert to opportunities to express appreciation and commendation.

Adapted from *Great Commission Breakthrough: "How to" Ideas for Great Commission Churches* (Nashville: The Sunday School Board of the Southern Baptist Convention, 1992), 68.

54. (HOW TO) Conduct a Worker Commitment Service

Conduct a worker commitment service.
- Lead workers to feel that they are a vital part of a significant mission.
- Provide each worker with a vision of the mission of the church.
- Recognize all workers and their leadership positions.
- Develop unity among the workers.
- Encourage workers as the church body commits to pray for them as they seek to carry out their responsibilities.
- Bring about a deeper commitment among the church family as members become more educated about the work of the church.

Consider elements that contribute to an effective commitment service.

Worship leaders.—The worship leaders should include the pastor, music director, and minister of education (if the church has one).

Welcome.—This part of the service indicates the reason for this service. Ask the minister of education or chairman of deacons to lead this part of the worship and to include a brief explanation and welcome to guests.

Music.—Select a theme song or a familiar hymn that can be used throughout the year. Then, anytime it is sung, it can serve as a reminder to church leaders of the focus for the year, and encourage them in their work.

Prayer of commitment.—Consider having all workers come to the commitment, asking God for His direction and committing the leaders to a year of ministry.

Responsive reading.—For the workers, pastor, and members to read responsively is an excellent way to provide focus and unity for workers and members. Select key passages that remind readers of their responsibilities.

Worker Commitment Service

Welcome
Theme Song
Prayer
Special Music
Message by Pastor

Commissioning and Response of Workers:

Pastor: God in His wisdom gave each one of us gifts to carry on His work. "It was He who gave some to be apostles, some to be prophets, some to be evangelists, and some to be pastors and teachers, to prepare God's people for works of service, so that the body of Christ may be built up" (Eph. 4:11-12, NIV).

Workers: We thank God for the gifts He has given us.

Pastor: Our community offers untold opportunities to share the gospel of Christ, to reach out to each person in love, and to share the message, "that God was reconciling the world to himself in Christ, not counting men's sins against them. And he has committed to us the message of reconciliation" (2 Cor. 5:19, NIV).

Workers: We thank God for the message of salvation found in Jesus Christ and for the opportunity to share it.

Pastor: The Bible is the inspired Word of God and our guide for living. "All Scripture is God-breathed and is useful for teaching, rebuking, correcting, and training in righteousness, so that the man of God may be thoroughly equipped for every good work" (2 Tim.3:16-17, NIV).

Workers: We thank God for His Holy Word.

Pastor: As leaders in our church, you have a sacred responsibility to reach, teach, equip, and minister to those assigned to you in whatever role you have. Whatever your responsibility, it is a sacred trust from God. "Now it is required that those who have been given a trust must prove faithful" (1 Cor. 4:2, NIV).

Workers: We recognize our great responsibility and commit ourselves to be faithful in it.

Prayer of Commitment by Pastor

Depart to Serve

Adapted from "How to Conduct a Worker Commitment Service," *Great Commission Breakthrough: "How to" Ideas for Great Commission Churches* (Nashville: The Sunday School Board of the Southern Baptist Convention, 1992), 113.

Encourage workers to use individual and small-group studies to continue work toward their Christian Growth Study Plan diplomas.–Ask workers to read a chapter each week in a good training resource. Report and discuss during your workers planning meeting.

Make books and tapes available, from the church media library, to workers for home and individual study.

Invite a group of workers to cooperate on completing a training book.– A different member of the group can focus on each chapter and complete the study questions at the end of that chapter. Then the group can come together for each person to report on their chapter. Remember, each person should read the entire book.

Publicly recognize workers who have earned Leadership Diplomas.– Take time during a Sunday morning worship service to tell the congregation about the excellent work done by some of their church leaders. Tell of the hours they have invested in making themselves better teachers and leaders. Present the diploma. Another way to recognize workers is to have a worker appreciation banquet at the end of the church year. Some smaller church pastors even prepare the meal themselves. Make volunteer workers feel important and appreciated.

56. (HOW TO) Develop a Church Constitution and Bylaws

Does a church need a constitution and bylaws?–Many churches have operated for years without these documents. These groups, however, usually acted and expressed themselves by some agreement. The written statement of this agreement is the essence of a constitution and bylaws.

Regulations should be formulated and put into printed form for distribution to officers who might need them for reference. Items that refer to the name of an organization; the nature of its membership; the rules for the election of its officers and trustees, along with their duties and responsibilities; and the definition of a quorum make up the constitution and bylaws.

One of the main values of a constitution and bylaws is the opportunity it gives the church to look at itself; to redefine its purposes, objectives, and procedures; and to evaluate the effectiveness of its organizational structure. Many church members are unacquainted with the polity of a Baptist church. The study involved in drawing up or revising a church constitution and bylaws may become a helpful educational process for all members.

Adopting a constitution and bylaws will enable the church to determine how democratically it is functioning. It will give the church an opportunity to set up in orderly fashion the church committees, officers, and organizations so that clearly defined lines of responsibility are established.

Furthermore a constitution and bylaws which set forth the procedures for the orderly handling of the church and its business often prevent difficulties and personal misunderstandings from arising within the church family.

What should a church include in its constitution?
• A preamble, setting forth the purpose of the constitution.
• The name of the church–its official legal title. If the church is incorporated under this name, no other church can legally use that name in the state.
• The objectives of the church.
• The church doctrinal statement or articles of faith.
• Relationships–a statement of the church's relationships to other groups.
• Church covenant.[1]

What should a church include in its bylaws?
• Membership
  1. Qualifications for church members, and how they may be received.
  2. Voting rights of church members.

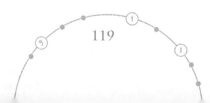

3. Termination of membership.

4. Discipline.

5. New member orientation.

6. Restoration.

• General Church Officers

1. Pastor.–How to call, duties, method of termination.

2. Other staff members.–Selection, duties, method of termination.

3. Deacons.–Number, how elected, term of office, duties, meetings.

4. Moderator.–How selected, duties.

5. Clerk.–How selected, duties.

6. Trustees.

7. Other needed officers.

• Program Services (recreation and media library).–How selected, duties.

• Church Committees

• Program Organizations

1. Sunday School.–Purpose, officers, how elected.

2. Discipleship Training.–Purpose, officers, how elected.

3. WMU.–Purpose, officers, how elected.

4. Brotherhood.–Purpose, officers, how elected.

5. Church Music Program.

6. Other needed organizations.

• Ordinances (procedures for conducting the church ordinances).

• Church Meetings

1. Worship.–Wednesday, Sunday.

2. Special services.–Revivals, study courses, officers, clinics, etc.

3. Regular business meetings.

4. Special business meetings.

5. Quorum.

6. Parliamentary rules.

• Church Finances (budget, accounting procedures).

• Church Operations Manual.

• Amendments (procedure for amending).

The constitution includes more permanent items regarding a church, such as the name, articles of faith, and church covenant. The bylaws are more flexible and are concerned with carrying out the purposes set forth in the constitution.

---

[1]See *The Baptist Hymnal* (Nashville: Convention Press, 1991), 476; James L. Sullivan, *Your Life and Your Church* (Nashville: Broadman Press, 1955), 42–43; *Encyclopedia of Southern Baptists*, Vol. 1:283.

57. (HOW TO) Develop Effective Policies

Given your existing situation, what should the church be doing? What policy statements are needed to fill in areas left undefined. Consider the following list of possible areas that might be included in facilities policy statements.

General Policies

1. Facility use, church function.
2. Facility use, nonchurch function.
3. Facility use by nonmembers.
4. Facility use for special events such as weddings, funerals, receptions.
5. Room arrangement.
6. Moving furniture and equipment.
7. Modifications to facilities.
8. Attachments to walls and structures.
9. Use of flammable, toxic, or corrosive items.
10. Use of open flame or candles.
11. Use of small electrical appliances.
12. Use of food preparation appliances in areas other than kitchen.
13. Maintenance contracts.
14. Maintenance schedules.
15. Decorator and color schemes.
16. Cleaning procedures.
17. Purchasing supplies.
18. Equipment and supplies.
19. Off-premises use of equipment and supplies.
20. Equipment replacement and addition schedules.
21. Security systems.
22. Safety and exterior security.
23. Insurance.
24. Handicapped access.
25. Security of personal items.
26. Safety and first aid.
27. Fire safety and evacuation.
28. Issuance and security of keys.
29. Parking lot maintenance.
30. The church sign.
31. Assignment of committee, staff, and employee personnel.
32. Energy conservation and control.
33. Fixed and semiportable sound and musical devices.
34. Installed telephone and data systems equipment.
35. Inventory and audit of plant accounting equipment.
36. Snow and ice removal.
37. Worship center and flower committee responsibilities.

Food Service Policies

1. Scheduling meals and events.
2. Authorized access to kitchen.
3. Access to pantry items.
4. Use of consumables for church-related events (paper plates, plasticware, etc.).
5. Use of kitchen items off premises.
6. Use of caterers.
7. Sunday morning coffee and confections.
8. Equipment inspection and maintenance.

9. Replacement and addition schedules.

10. Hot water and dishwasher inspection schedules.

11. Routine insecticide maintenance contracts.

12. Ordering, receipt, and accountability of supplies.

13. Wedding, reception, and special events.

14. Safety procedures.

Vehicle and Motorized Equipment

1. Scheduling of vehicles.

2. Authorized drivers.

3. Passengers (maximum/minimum numbers).

4. Passengers (member/nonmember procedures).

5. Inspection, maintenance, and upkeep schedules.

6. Cleanliness responsibilities.

7. Use by staff and employees.

8. Charges to credit cards.

9. Reimbursement for personal expenses.

10. Maximum mileage limitations.

11. Use of rental and for-hire vehicles.

12. Use of staff vehicles.

13. Use of maintenance vehicles.

14. Storage of flammable and combustible supplies.

15. Replacement schedules.

16. Insurance.

Many churches include preschool activities in facility policy statements. Others with recreation facilities include this special area in the policy formulation. Any church must select and include those areas that require policy statements for its own situation.

Write policy statements in clear and understandable language. Policy statements should be stated in terminology easily understood by church members who will acknowledge, approve, and function by them.

Effective policy statements should:
• Be a few short sentences in length.
• Address a few related topics in each statement.
• Be broad in scope.
• Assign responsibility for implementation and review.
• Be written in a positive rather than a punitive context.
• Encourage imagination and creativity in implementation.
• Not be unnecessarily restrictive.
• Be enforceable and legally defensible.
• Be developed with the assistance of the individual(s) or group(s) who must implement and use the policy.

Obtain the approval of the church. Policy statements should be presented to the church for acknowledgment, questioning, and final approval.

58. (HOW TO) Develop a Safety Policy for Preschoolers and Children

Providing Appropriate Screening Procedures

We live in a society where people sue one another, and most state courts no longer recognize the idea of "charitable immunity" for churches. Hundreds of churches have been sued during the past decade for injuries to children. Careful screening procedures are needed for all volunteers and employed preschool and children's leaders and teachers.

Recommended steps to protect children and teachers include the use of screening forms, personal interviews, and background checks. Consult your church's attorney and insurance company to adapt for your use the screening form information.

You need to keep on file a release form signed by all teachers permitting you to conduct reference and background checks. You also need written documentation of contacts you make with references and information you discuss in the personal interview. All of this information is confidential and must be kept filed in a secure area.

Other Safeguards for Protecting Preschoolers and Children:

• Two or more teachers with each group of preschoolers and children at all times.
• A small window in classroom doors giving a view of the entire room.
• Protective procedures for changing diapers and assisting in rest rooms.
• A security method for releasing preschoolers to authorized adults only.
• Specified policies for immediate reporting of any suspected child abuse.
• Ongoing supervision and training for all teachers.

Screening Form

Prepare a form which meets your needs. The form might include: date; full name, address, and phone number; photo ID and/or driver's license number; prior church membership; volunteer work; all prior work with preschoolers and children; three references, including addresses and phone numbers; and a statement of any prior convictions for abuse, molestation, or crimes against minors.

For many churches the form will include a dated, signed, and witnessed release from the potential teacher which states he/she is providing correct information; authorizes the references and churches listed to provide information and opinions regarding his/her fitness for working with children; releases all parties from liability for furnishing information; waives the right to inspect the response of references; grants permission for church leaders to conduct a criminal background check; and agrees to be bound by the policies and bylaws of the church.

Personal Interview

Prior to the personal interview, contact all references and check on the person's former work and volunteer situations relating to children. Maintain confidential records of responses from those you contact. During the interview jot down the person's responses regarding Christian testimony, special interest in working with preschoolers and children, past teaching and volunteer experience, interest in receiving training, and other such information. Consult with your church's attorney for help with all aspects of the screening process, including the questions you ask, the forms you use, and the confidential records you maintain.

When appropriate procedures are consistently followed, your church is in a position to protect preschoolers and children, safeguard teachers, and reduce the legal liability of your church. Assure potential teachers that their cooperation with the screening process helps your church meet moral, spiritual, and legal responsibilities with loving diligence.

Follow-Up on Enlistment Contacts

Check back with the prospective leader in two or three days, as agreed upon. If the person agrees to accept the position, thank him and discuss further steps, such as turning in the completed screening forms, and scheduling a short personal interview. Prior to the interview, check the references and other background information, jotting down results of the contacts. During the interview, use suggestions outlined above in the personal interview with space to record information discussed. File all forms in a secure area.

59. (HOW TO) Conduct a Risk Management Assessment

What you don't know can hurt you!

To understand risk management, you must first know what a tort is. A *tort* is defined as "a wrongful act for which a civil action will take place." This wrongful act can be in the form of an omission (something not done that should have been), or of commission (something that was done that should not have been done). This action is initiated by the person(s) harmed usually for negligent behavior. If the victim can prove that the agency or the person in charge was negligent in carrying out his duties, and that there is a direct cause between legal duty and the resulting loss or injury, and that an actual loss or injury occurred, a legal proceeding may follow.

Any church or individual can be sued if:
• They direct, ratify, or condone negligent acts.
• They practice incompetent hiring.
• They don't have job descriptions or have inadequate job descriptions.
• They practice insufficient staff training.
• There is unclear establishment or enforcement of rules.
• They fail to comply with laws or corporate policy.
• They fail to remedy dangerous conditions.
• They fail to give notice of unsafe conditions.

A risk management plan takes a close look at policies, procedures, and practices. Taking this kind of proactive approach can protect against undue risk and serve as a deterrent to suits by showing evidence of intent to act responsibly as you tried to foresee problems. To begin to implement a risk management plan a church will:

1. Designate one person to be responsible.
2. This person is authorized to:
    • Identify risk factors.
    • Work with committees on insurance needs, safety equipment needs, etc.
    • Stay informed by attending conferences, getting up-to-date literature.
    • Establish reporting procedures.
    • Work with and train staff.
    • Work with trustees; legal, insurance, and local code authorities.
    • Set certification standards.
    • Call attention to potential problem areas.

Often the courts have looked favorably on certain practices that show prudent actions were taken to lessen risks to participants. *Risk Management* lists 16 characteristics of a risk management plan. These steps can be adapted to any church. Seek the counsel of your attorney when planning any legal action.

Steps in Developing a Risk Management Plan

1. Develop philosophy, theology, and policies for your church.
2. Assess the liability needs of programs.
3. Write down goals and objectives of your ministries.
4. Be conscious of liabilities during development of ministries, programs, and facilities.
5. Develop programs and ministries.
6. Provide proper supervision.
7. Establish regulations, policies, and procedures.
8. Do regular safety inspections.
9. Analyze accident-reporting procedures.
10. Develop emergency procedures.
11. Develop releases, waivers, and agreements.
12. Check insurance coverages.
13. Train volunteers, staff, leaders.
14. Practice good public relations.
15. Enlist outside legal and insurance specialists.
16. Review risk management plan periodically.[1]

Jesus said that we are to "love our neighbor as ourselves." If this is true, this love must manifest itself in being morally responsible for the care and well-being of all who participate in our ministry. People have a right to expect the utmost in care and concern. Providing prudent, reasonable care includes looking for any and all possibilities of harm. It means providing the best and safest programming, equipment, and facilities possible. Loving others means taking on the moral responsibility of caring for their safety—not because the law says we must but because it is the right thing to do. Risk management is your responsibility. The size of the church makes no difference.

By John Garner, director, Ministry Team Leadership Department, LifeWay Church Resources, Nashville, Tennessee.

[1]James A. Peterson, *Risk Management for Park, Recreation and Leisure Services* (Champaign, IL: Management Learning Laboratories, 1992).

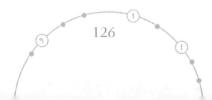

60. HOW TO Understand and Use Parliamentary Procedure

Paul said, "Let all things be done decently and in order" (1 Cor. 14:40). Most churches today use *Robert's Rules of Order* to try to comply with Paul's advice. Underlying the traditions and practices of every congregation are basic principles meant to guarantee that decisions made in business meetings will be fair and reflect the majority. You probably need to have a copy of *Robert's Rules* for reference, but here are 10 tips. Observing them will eliminate most problems that arise during business meetings.

1. Don't get personal when differences of opinion arise.—Arguments on a personal level are always out of order. Limit discussion to the pros and cons of the subject on the floor. The moderator should rule out of order any comment that questions the motives or competence of another member.

2. Don't take sides on controversial matters while presiding.—Usually, the presiding officer in a meeting is to remain neutral and make sure both sides of an issue are treated fairly. Normally, the moderator does not make motions, express personal opinion, or vote (except in a tie). If the pastor serves as moderator, as is best in most smaller to medium-size churches, living by the letter of this law may be difficult. Sometimes guidance from the pastor is needed. If he is serving as moderator, it is usually acceptable for him to comment, with common consent of the body. Or the moderator can relinquish the chair to someone else and provide needed leadership. Most churches, most of the time, agree that the pastor who serves as moderator may comment and still preside.

3. Don't end discussion arbitrarily.—Everyone has a right to be heard in any democratic body. The rules provide that discussion can be ended by two-thirds majority vote or by general (that is unanimous) consent. The fact that someone has "called for the question" does not necessarily mean that all discussion must end. It simply means that the body will vote on whether to end discussion and move to the question. Of course, the wise moderator may say, "If there is no further discussion (pausing to permit anyone to speak), we will proceed with the vote."

4. Don't get sidetracked.—Limit discussion to the pending motion. Amendments can get confusing, so make notes, if necessary, and stay on the item before the body. Discuss the amendment, vote on it, then return discussion to the original motion.

5. Don't hold special meetings without notice.—All members have the right to know of special, important decisions. You could win the battle but lose the war with this kind of unfair tactic.

6. Abide by the bylaws of the church.—If bylaws are unduly restrictive or unfair, change them. But, while they are in effect, abide by them.

7. Be certain to make motions abundantly clear.—Business meetings can be confusing. Pause before the vote to state clearly the motion before the body. If voting on an amendment, state the amendment clearly and explain that the vote is only on the amendment, not the motion.

8. On the other hand, in most churches, it is not necessary to insist on trivial technicalities.

9. Be sure that accurate minutes are kept.—Memory is not sufficient when important or controversial decisions are before the body.

10. Do your homework.—Before the meeting, think through possible questions, responses, emotions, etc. As much as possible, be prepared for any situation.

61. (HOW TO) Report Suspected Child Abuse

Reporting suspected abuse or neglect of children by their parents is always a tricky situation. When they are church members, it is especially difficult. Even though a minister is legally and morally bound to call when child abuse is suspected, the issue remains complicated. Questions persist: How does one know exactly when to call? What will the agency do? Will the child be at greater risk after the call? What if the parent discovers someone at the church made the call? Will doors to ministry be closed if they learn that the pastor placed the call? This situation will never be easy, but here are some steps to help you through the process.

The Call

Doing what is best for the child is always right. Blatant signs of child abuse would certainly get attention, and the decision to call would be easy. But not many cases are so obvious.

Do not interrogate a child.—This could later be misconstrued as an attempt to mislead a child into making false statements, or it might scare a child needlessly. Do investigate the situation, however. Talk with teachers and leaders who regularly come in contact with the child and other members of the family. Have others noticed a change in behavior? Are reasons known for the changes?

Laws vary in every state about what constitutes abuse or neglect. When in doubt, it is best to call. If the report does not fit the state's definition, at least the issue will be clarified.

Where action is needed quickly, call the police.—They respond faster than child protection agencies. Local phone books should have information about whom to call, or call the appropriate number at the end of this article.

Legally the call must include only names, addresses, and allegations. A more helpful report includes any available information on the family and as much specific information about the abuse or neglect as possible.

The Response

Making the call is not the end of responsibility. The agency may not believe an investigation is warranted, or they may find no abuse or neglect. Those who see the child regularly must continue to monitor the situation. If abuse is discovered, members of the church will need to support the child and the new caregivers while trying to understand parental needs as they get help.

The Church's Role

Those who work with children can give them unconditional love and under-standing. They can direct the child to esteem-building activities and those that teach self-preservation.

The church can also help parents by putting them in touch with community agencies for counseling, providing classes in child-rearing techniques, or helping them find support groups. Preventative classes to educate and support parents are the best opportunity not to have to make this kind of intervention call.

The Aftermath

Most experts agree that the best plan is to tell parents before making a report. This conversation should communicate a desire to get help for the entire family. It should build on a ministry rapport that is already evident. Parents know that the church is legally bound to make the call. Reminding them of this and offering to help them can pave the way for ministry.

Even if the parents become angry and threaten to leave the church, the action is necessary for the good of the child and the family. The goal is to improve family relationships in the long run.

Resource Numbers

Agency	What They Do
Parents Anonymous **(800) 421-0353**	24-hour hotline for parents who are having problems dealing with their children. They provide community referrals and will listen to those needing to talk.
Boys Town **(800) 448-3000**	24-hour number for children or adults to call regarding problematic issues.
National Referral Network **(800) KID-SAVE**	Provides referrals to local resources and agencies.
Child Help USA **(800) 422-4453**	Helps callers determine appropriate agency to call when reporting abuse or neglect.
National Clearinghouse on Family Support and Children's Mental Health Family Resources **(800) 628-1696**	Provides referrals to local community agencies and informational resources for both parents and professionals.

62. (HOW TO) Conduct an Effective Committee or Team Meeting

Pastors invest a lot of time in meetings. Most meetings are too long. That wouldn't be too bad, except that they are also ineffective.

Plan the meeting well.—Planning is really simple. It is determining where you are going and how you will get there. Below are steps in planning a meeting.

Determine the need for the meeting.—If there is no need, the meeting should not take place. What are the apparent needs? How is each need related to the team or committee? Does the need demand a meeting, or could one person handle the problem? What will happen or not happen if a meeting is not held?

State the purpose of the meeting.—The leader of the team or committee should state the purpose of the meeting. The purpose may be stated in the form of a goal. For example, "The purpose of this meeting is to develop a process for training our Sunday School workers." One advantage could be that stating a purpose may limit the scope of the meeting. If team members begin to "chase rabbits," the leader can call them back to the purpose. Some possible purposes are:

- Receiving reports.
- Defining, analyzing, or solving reports.
- Sharing information.
- Gaining acceptance of an idea.
- Reconciling differing views.

Schedule the meeting.—If the church has policies about meeting times and places, check with those who handle the church calendar to schedule the meeting.

Plan the meeting agenda.—An agenda can serve as guideline to move toward the accomplishment of its purpose. The agenda should be shared with the team or committee before the meeting. This will help team members prepare and know how much time to set aside for the meeting. A good agenda will include the following:

- Date, place, and time of meeting.
- Subject(s) for discussion.
- Background statements.

• Present condition of subject.
• Purpose and aim of meeting.

Arrange for facilities.—The facilities needed will be determined by the purpose and size of the meeting. It is best if the room is not so large the group gets lost in it. This makes discussion difficult. Most team or committee meetings are best conducted with members sitting in a circle or semi-circle.

Make assignments.—Advance assignments will help a team move to its conclusion quickly and efficiently.

Get started right.
• Start on time. Don't punish those who made the sacrifice to arrive on time by delaying the meeting.
• State the purpose of the meeting.
• Ask someone to pray that God will lead the group to achieve the purpose of the meeting.

Stay on track.—Most team or committee meetings that don't stay on track are ineffective. Most of the time, a chairman or team leader should not allow too much discussion of non-agenda items.
• Limit discussion to agenda items.
• Summarize key points.
• Reach conclusion as soon as possible.

Involve all members.—Here are a few suggestions to help the leader involve members.
• Ask open-ended questions.
• Distribute questions in advance of meeting.
• Use a brainstorm approach.

Complete the meeting.—This step is just as important as beginning the meeting well. As the meeting is concluded, review all decisions and list unresolved problems.

Evaluate the meeting.—This must be done to improve future meetings. Evaluation is not criticism or faultfinding. It is pinpointing the strong and weak points of a meeting and searching for ways to improve.

Adapted from James Sheffield, *Church Officer and Committee Guidebook* (Nashville: Convention Press, 1976), 87–100.

63. (HOW TO) Make Wise Decisions

As a pastor, you must make many decisions. Much of the pastor's time
and energy are consumed by the decision-making process. Some decisions
can be made easily and cause little difficulty. Others are crucial and have
significant consequences. Here are some factors to keep in mind as you
approach the many decisions you must make.

The Responsibility Factor

Some decisions a pastor must make are exclusively in his domain. Others
require him to involve other people in the decision-making process.
Confusion can result when a decision is made by the wrong person or
group. In general, people who are to share in the consequences of a
decision should be involved in making that decision. Also people are
more likely to feel responsible for the results of a decision if they have
had a part in making it.

The Urgency Factor

Decisions that are not crucial should not require more time or energy than
necessary. Ask, "What would happen if nothing were done?" On the other
hand, crucial decisions should not be neglected.

The Time Factor

This refers to the amount of time allowed before the decision must be
made. Decisions that have far-reaching impact should not be made impul-
sively. On the other hand, never neglect a decision that must be made in a
timely fashion. Be careful that procrastination does not become a factor.

A Model for Decision-Making

Clarify the Issue
This is essential. Your judgment can be distorted if you do not clearly see the issues.

Gather Information
Take enough time to gather needed information. Consult with experts or caring friends. Do your homework.

Explore Alternatives and Consequences
Several actions could be taken. What would be the probable result of each? Consider all the possibilities.

Pray for Guidance
To emphasize the necessity of prayer is more than a pious reminder. Decision-making calls for wisdom. Only God can give true wisdom. God is more concerned about you and your church than you can imagine. Consult Him.

Adapted from Brooks Faulkner, *Getting on Top of Your Work* , *A Manual for the 21st-Century Minister,* (Nashville: Convention Press, 1999).

64. (HOW TO) Be Certain Buildings and Equipment Are Properly Maintained

Whether your church has a full-time custodian, a volunteer custodian, or something in between, making certain all the buildings and equipment are properly cleaned and cared for can be a challenge. Here are two checklists that may be helpful.

Washroom Maintenance Guide

1. Load service cart and move to washroom.
2. Flush toilets and urinals.
3. Empty urinal strainers.
4. Force water from bowl with mop.
5. Apply cleaner inside toilet bowls and urinals.
6. Empty and clean waste receptacles.
7. Dyst air vents, light fixtures, window frames, and toilet partitions.
8. Clean mirrors.
9. Check soap dispenser valves for proper operation.
10. Wash exterior of soap dispensers.
11. Spot clean walls and partitions.
12. Clean wash basins, faucets, and other surfaces.
13. Polish fixtures.
14. Clean pipes under wash basins and other fixtures.
15. Scrape gum and dry deposits from floor.
16. Sweep floor with push broom or treated mop.
17. Clean inside of toilets and urinals.
18. Prepare fresh cleaning solution.
19. Clean outside of toilets and urinals.
20. Rinse toilet seats.
21. Check/refill all dispensers: soap, towel, toilet tissue, sanitary napkins.
22. Replace urinal and toilet deodorant b locks, if used.
23. Remove supply cart from washroom.
24. Clear floor for mopping.
25. Soak area around toilets and urinals with cleaning solution.
26. Begin mopping floor farthest from entrance.
27. Clean baseboard.
28. Take mopping equipment to waste sink, empty bucket, rinse, and wipe dry or drain.

29. Rinse, clean, and wring out mops, cloths, and sponges.
30. Hang mop, head down, to dry.
31. Spread cloths, store sponges for drying.

Sample Schedule for Continuing Building and Equipment Inspection		
Month	**Areas of Inspection**	**Maintenance Needs**
January	Complete church auditorium, chapel, baptistry, vestibules	
February	Church offices, media center	
March	Kitchen and dining areas	
April	All outdoor areas— parking lots, lawn, plantings, walkways, signs	
May	All preschool departments and play areas	
June	All children's departments	
July	All youth departments and recreation areas	
August	All adult departments, hallways, and exits	
September	Roof, steeple, gutters, and drains; all exterior surfaces	
October	All closets, storage areas, stairs and fire escapes	
November	Plumbing system and all fixtures; all drinking fountains; fire-fighting equipment	
December	Electrical system— main box, all outlets, switches, fixtures, and appliances	

Adapted from Tim J. Holcomb, compiler, *A Maintenance Management Manual for Southern Baptist Churches* (Nashville: Convention Press, 1990), 17, 30.

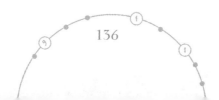

65. (HOW TO) Organize the Books in Your Personal Library

The system that works for me is not the same as you would find at the city library or your church media library. This method of organizing your books is built from years of experience as a pastor and reflects the way I use my books. I am simply not a person who is likely to label each book with numbers and letters according to subject or title. I place my books in groups according to the way I use them.

Books of the Bible.—The heart of a pastor's library must be books that are used for Bible study. Over the years, I have found that most large, multi-volume commentaries are less practical than smaller, single volume resources. If I were just starting my library, I would consider purchasing Broadman & Holman's *The New American Commentary*. It is helpful, practical, conservative, and scholarly.

The logical way to organize these books is by order of Bible books. Start with Genesis and go through Revelation. Place commentaries on the Old Testament before Genesis, and the New Testament before Matthew.

Other Bible study books.—Bible study books that relate to more than one particular book of the Bible come next on your shelves. For example, your Greek and Hebrew books will be in this group. Also place Bible histories, Bible dictionaries, etc. in this group.

Subject-related groups.—If you are organizing an existing library, a quick look at your books will reveal these groups. If you are organizing for a library to be acquired in the future, consider the kinds of subjects that will be interesting or helpful. You will certainly have or want to acquire several books on prayer. The same is true for the Holy Spirit, spiritual gifts, angels, demons, end times, etc. Placing these subject groups together on the shelf will be sufficient to allow you to view and find them at will.

People in the Bible.—Arrange books on Bible characters in order of their occurrence in Scripture—Abraham, Moses, David, the prophets, Jesus, Peter, Paul, etc.

Biographies.—There is much to learn from heroes, leaders, and others about whom biographies are written. Some are positive examples; others are negative. Some sermon illustrations can be found in their life stories.

Leadership.—Every effective pastor is an effective leader. Many leadership skills are needed to face the various challenges that come to every pastor. Learn from business leaders, religious leaders, and others. Use this group of books often.

Church growth and Sunday School growth.—This group of books will be filled with useful resources. Remember that a growing church or Sunday School is reaching people and teaching them the Word of God. It's not about numbers; it's about people. Within this group, pull together smaller classifications. Some books will relate to pastors leading their churches to grow; others will be for smaller churches. Some will provide help for an age group within the church.

Other groups of books.—As you build or organize your library, other groups will emerge. Arrange the books on the shelf with others of like kind. Books of sermons may be helpful as you see how other pastors deal with a certain passage, for example.

This simple system of organizing the books in a library has been helpful for me. I can find any book I need, and I am free to locate the books I use most near my desk.

66. (HOW TO) Use Time Wisely

Time managed means time saved—that is, more time for pastoral ministry, growth, study, and family. The keys for "redeeming the time" concern priorities, procrastination, and plans.

Assign Priorities

Yes, "to everything there is a . . . time" (Eccl. 3:1). But not all matters and events have equal importance. Assign priorities to guide how valuable time should be spent. For example, a daily schedule may give high priority to intercessory prayer and to funeral sermon preparation and low priority to getting a haircut and attending a local service club meeting. Label the high priority items as *A* and the low priority items as *C*. Sort the *A* items by importance and schedule time to accomplish them. Do *C* items when *A* items have been done satisfactorily (watch for the trap of feeling good about doing several *C* items which really matter little).

Avoid Procrastination

Since we do not know "what shall be on the morrow" (Jas. 4:14), avoid putting off working on *A* items. Procrastination behaviors include day-dreaming (not the same as mental brainstorming), socializing (not the same as pastoral visitation), and getting organized by making "to do" lists (not the same as planning). Procrastination is often a product of dread, fear, fatigue, lack of interest, or a quest for perfection. Overcome putting off by getting started (some work on *A* items is better than none) and by breaking large tasks into smaller portions. Focus on the goal and not on just the "having to get there."

Amend Plans

"Plan your work, and work your plan" does not imply rigidity. Pastoral priorities change due to unexpected deaths, family emergencies, or personal illness. Some matters or events lead to others. Plan for the unexpected by avoiding procrastination and by amending plans due to changing priorities. Consider the situation, your options, the consequences of each option, and adjust accordingly. Let the flexibility, which keeps skyscrapers from breaking in storms, keep you from breaking in the "storms" of stressful developments and demands.

Time management can make a difference in whether time is spent or used. Listing events in a pocket planner or on a desk calendar is helpful; but assigning priorities, avoiding procrastination, and amending plans help manage time effectively. Save time by managing time. And always remember the time management prayer of Moses: "So teach us to number our days" (Ps. 90:12).

By Jerry Barlow, chairman, General Education Department, College of Undergraduate Studies, New Orleans Baptist Theological Seminary. Dr. Barlow is qualified not only by his experience and study as a professor but also by his many years of service as a pastor. His work is practical and comes from a pastor's heart.

Resources

Rainer, Thom S. *Eating the Elephant: Bite-sized Steps to Achieve Long-Term Growth in Your Church.* Nashville: Broadman & Holman Publishers, 1994.

Randall, Robert L. *The Time of Your Life: Self–Time Management for Pastors.* Nashville: Abingdon Press, 1994.

67. **HOW TO** Use the Telephone to Maximize Your Time

When my family and I first moved to the community in which I now live, we visited Immanuel Baptist Church. Several people from the church visited our home, and that was nice, but another kind of contact really impressed us. The pastor of that church, Donald Owens, called us on the phone every Saturday morning for several weeks. Those phone calls made an impact on us, and we really came to look forward to them.

I am not suggesting that you stop going into people's homes. I am not suggesting that you abandon personal visitation and use the telephone exclusively. It is, however, worthwhile for pastors to contact several dozen people in the same amount of time it would take to visit two. Here are a few tips about using the phone to make the most of your time.

Set aside a time each week to make phone calls.—Unless there is a real emergency, honor this commitment. Consider two to three hours each week for intentional phoning. Time spent answering the phone during the week doesn't count. This is time for phone contacting which you initiate and in which you control the agenda. If you choose Saturday morning (like my pastor), don't start too early. Depending on your community, 9:00 a.m. is probably about right.

Begin this time with prayer.—Ask God to bless your time spent on the phone. You would never go out on visitation without prayer, so don't begin this outreach time without prayer.

Give high priority to your newest prospects.—Those who visited your services last Sunday or who have recently been added to your prospect list need this contact from the pastor. By the way, if this Saturday morning phone call is your first contact with a prospect who visited your services last Sunday, you have waited too late. See 80. "How to Develop an Effective 12-Month Outreach Plan."

Keep a list of those you are developing as telephone prospects.—Make a note of when you call and the response. Depending on the prospect and your priorities, decide how often to call each family on your list.

Some of your church members need contact from their pastor, and will appreciate these phone calls more than a visit. Use some of your telephone time to minister to members. Remember, the telephone can't totally replace personal visitation.

Personalize every contact.—Talk to and about the children in the family. Call the names of family members. Parents appreciate someone who knows their children and calls them by name. If you are like me, you will need lots of information at your fingertips. Keep the prospect cards, your personal records, and other bits of information about the prospect nearby so you can provide that vital personal touch.

Remind your congregation that telephone contacts are a significant outreach strategy.—When a prospect family joins your church, mention the phone calls. This will help your congregation see the value of their pastor's spending time this way.

Spend a few minutes on Sunday afternoon calling those who visit your services on Sunday morning.—You can do this while you watch football. Get the TV remote in one hand and your telephone in the other and use the "mute" button while you talk on the phone. That Sunday afternoon call from the pastor makes a great impression on first-time guests. Tell them you were happy to see them in your services, and offer to answer any questions. Ask them when that week you or someone from your staff might come by for a visit. Be cordial and warm.

68. (HOW TO) Teach Lifestyle Stewardship

Teach stewardship as a lifestyle because teaching it any other way will not produce a changed life or changed priorities. Nor will it result in a commitment to put God first in every area of life.

The consequences of not teaching lifestyle stewardship are evident. There is a growing unrest among Baptists who feel unfulfilled in service, clearly hungry to be actively engaged in giving—not just of their money but also their time and talents—to the cause of Christ.

Step 1.—Create a climate in your church that regularly confronts your people with God's Word regarding the management of their assets—time, financial resources, and personal gifts. Make sure the climate is both positive and healthy, and support it with prayer.[1]

Step 2.—Establish clearly—through preaching, teaching, personal example, and church practice—that there is great joy, deep peace, and enormous satisfaction in putting God first in every area of life. Pastor, staff, and lay leaders should model Christian stewardship. The church itself must conduct its own business, its own giving, and its own outreach according to biblical models.

Step 3.—Provide the Christian asset manager with the tools needed to be successful. People were not born knowing how to manage resources. It is an acquired skill, and specific learning activities are needed to equip individuals and families to be effective stewards.[2]

Step 4.—Produce a continuous flow of preaching, teaching, learning activities and practical experiences that educate the congregation. Avoid at all costs the temptation to focus on only the financial aspects of stewardship. To emphasize pledging a budget and tithing, apart from issues of the heart, is to rob the people of God's clear teaching that He is interested above all else in our heart condition.[2] The best way to avoid misunderstanding on this point is to develop a year-round calendar with stewardship elements every quarter of the year.[3] Integrate stewardship concepts and education into every area of church life, and clearly define the implications of faithful stewardship among all age groups.

Step 5.–Preach and teach clearly that stewardship is first and foremost a heart issue. Teaching a person to tithe purely from a legalistic approach is to cheat him of the knowledge that God is the greatest giver of all time. Our giving, then, is simply a response to His giving and becomes the way by which we express our love and thanks for what He did for us.

Step 6.–Make a concerted effort to educate the entire body of believers about the dangers of debt. You have only to pick up today's paper to see again that our nation is wallowing in red ink. Christians are not immune to the consumer debt crisis that is sweeping our country. Give your people financial management tools that reveal the crippling effects of debt, the dangers it presents to marriages and homes, and the opportunities that are lost when a family is slave to the lender.[4]

Step 7.–Help your people discover their gifts. Show your people how to find out the ways God gifts each of His children with skills, talents, and spiritual gifts.Then encourage them to use and develop those gifts within the body of Christ and the local community. Conduct short classes year-round, encouraging every member to attend. Those that have discovered their gifts can share and encourage, while those who have not can be led to see who they are in Christ–special, unique, and equipped for service.

In short, preach, teach, and model a lifestyle stewardship that is so winsome and so compelling that your members will want to emulate that lifestyle and in so doing, will bring glory to God!

Adapted from an article by Norma J. Goldman, Managing Director, Church Leadership Publishing, LifeWay Christian Resources, Nashville, Tennessee.

Resources

Successful Christian Financial Management (a seminar). Call 615-251-2808 for more information.

---

[1]Larry Burkett, *How Much Is Enough?* (Nashville: LifeWay Christian Resources, 1999).
[2]Mary Hunt and Yvonne Burrage, *The Financially Confident Woman Module* (Nashville: Convention Press, 1997).
[3]*ABCs of Church Budgeting and Promotion* (Nashville: Convention Press, 1997).
[4]Successful Christian Financial Management (a seminar), for more information call LifeWay Christian Resources (615) 251-5750

69. (HOW TO) Decide Whether to Purchase Your Own Home

Is home ownership right for you? If you have an opportunity to choose your own housing, should you buy? Here are several factors to weigh as you consider purchasing a home.

Money for Down Payment
The source of money for a down payment needs to come from your own funds. Save the money. Of course, some churches offer no-interest loans, which can be good or bad. I do not recommend borrowing money for a down payment on a home. Borrowed money, whatever the source, must be repaid. If the church lends you the money, you have an obligation to the church beyond your obligation as a minister. Parents and family may provide funds as a gift. There are also federal laws governing potential sources of money for a down payment.

The Price of the Home
Determine how much housing allowance the church is providing. The housing allowance may include enough to make the payments plus utilities, furniture, and other needs. Find the right neighborhood for you. How quickly homes sell in that neighborhood may be a factor.

Insufficient Income or Housing Allowance
The money for the house you want may not be sufficiently allocated in your total salary package. It is best to limit the cost of your home purchase to approximately two times your yearly salary package, not including retirement and insurance.

If you and your spouse work, the tendency is to buy a house based on both salaries. It is best to buy based on one salary. You may stretch a little, but it is best not to depend on two salaries because it places unneeded pressure on your family.

Need to Pay Off Other Bills First

Before you buy a home, you need to pay off all credit cards or like-kind debts. Get your total debt down to below 36 percent of your before-deductions salary, based on one income.

Credit problems could restrict purchase.—Obtain a copy of your credit report. The bank your church uses will most likely help you with that. If there are problems on your report, correct them before making a loan application.

Anticipate moving.—If you anticipate that you may move from your church within three to five years, it is usually best not to buy a home. If you do not buy, but determine to rent, save a certain amount of each paycheck designated for the future purchase of a home. You may ask your church to consider providing increased housing allowance designated for the purchase of a home.

By J. David Carter, now retired, at the time of this writing, consultant, Church Stewardship Services, LifeWay Church Resources, Nashville, Tennessee.

70. (HOW TO) Purchase Your Own Home

Living in a house owned by the church is an interesting experience. People may feel free to drop by unannounced. You may feel pressured to decorate according to the wishes of the church. And you may always have that uneasy sense that you are renting from the church.

Many pastors today have the opportunity to purchase their own homes. Once you have decided that purchasing a home is best for you, here are a few tips.

Educate yourself about home buying.—Learn enough to be able to carry on a conversation. This knowledge is not intended to be a substitute for using a buyer/broker as your agent.

Drive through area neighborhoods and look for a well-maintained location. Choose a neighborhood as well as a house.

Accumulate the down payment and closing costs.—The Federal Housing Administration (FHA) is designed to help persons buy a home. While they do not provide the loan, they insure the loan in case the buyer defaults. You can get into a home for as little as 5 percent, including all costs. A conventional loan will require approximately 10 percent of the purchase price in out-of-pocket money to get into the house. Some banks will lend church staff members money to buy a home because of the relationship the church has with the bank.

Evaluate your needs and desires.—There is a difference between what you need and what you would like to have. Discuss these needs and desires with your spouse. You may be more concerned about the school district and distance to the church, shopping, and hospitals than the particular house. You may want a newer house but discover that all your needs can be met in a well-maintained older home.

Find a buyer/broker.—You need someone to represent you who is on your side. The agent who lists the home for sale has a legal obligation to represent the seller, not the buyer. It is the practice in many areas for the seller to pay the commission for the buyer's real estate agent. So, most likely, it will not cost you anything to have your own agent.

Get preapproved for a mortgage.—*Preapproval* and *prequalified* are similar-sounding terms with different meanings. *Preapproval* means that the lender will lend you the money when you find the right house. To be prequalified is to know how much you can afford. You have more negotiating power when you are preapproved. The seller can be more confident of a sale with a buyer who is preapproved.

Find a home and make an offer.—Notice the sequence of this process, where actually finding the right house fits. While moving to a new church, a trip to find a home is usually part of the move. The trip is usually rushed with several other things on the schedule. It is best to make a trip solely for the purpose of finding a house. Your buyer/broker can help you find a lender that can preapprove you even though you live a long distance away. Today, some use the Internet to find a lender.

Hire a professional inspector for existing homes.—Once you find the home, hire a professional inspector. Write a contingency into the contract, giving you the right to wait until you are satisfied with the inspector's report before you finalize the contract. Do not ask someone from the church to inspect the house. As you search for a home, do so with integrity. Avoid any expectations of generosity from church members. Ask God to help you make this decision with wisdom. Follow the advice of your real estate agent. Do not hesitate to ask questions and wait for satisfactory answers.

The purchase of a home is one of the most important decisions of your lifetime; make it wisely, and enjoy your new home. By the way, when you move from the parsonage to your own home, feel free to put as many nail holes in the walls as you wish, and paint the kitchen any color you like.

By J. David Carter, now retired, at the time of this writing, consultant, Church Stewardship Services, LifeWay Church Resources, Nashville, Tennessee.

71. (HOW TO) Handle Church Financial Matters with Integrity

Eight practical steps can help protect lay and staff members from any hint of impropriety and increase members' confidence in the way the church handles the Lord's money.

1. Establish a committee—not a single individual—to place church offerings in bank night deposit bags.—(Many churches use the usher committee to handle this responsibility.) Designate one individual to lock the bag in the presence of at least two or more committee members. Establish a secure location in the church where the keys are kept.

2. Make arrangements with your bank to place the locked bag in the bank night depository for safekeeping.—(Never send money home with an individual.) Rotate among committee members the responsibility for taking the bag for deposit. The committee chairman or his designate should pick up the bag Monday for counting by members of the committee. The committee should sign the register tapes and deposit slips, verifying the deposit before taking the money to the bank for deposit.

3. Establish policies to ensure that people who handle church monies are different from the ones charged with spending it.

4. Establish a policy requiring at least two signatures on checks.—Make it a practice to give this responsibility to people who are thoroughly familiar with the budget and church spending policies. Never assign this responsibility to an individual who would be inclined to sign without questioning. Only one church staff member should be a check signer. It is best to have a committee of at least three others who can sign for the second signature.

5. Minimize the number of discretionary funds or accounts.—Too many such accounts discourage people from giving to a unified budget and may result in underfunding other areas.

6. At the beginning of the church year, set out clearly what is to be done with surplus funds (money) given above the budget or budgeted funds not spent.—Some churches choose to apply surplus funds to debt retirement. This policy reaffirms there is accountability and ethical spending habits, leading church members to know that excess funds will be used wisely.

7. Special program offerings (revivals, concerts, seminars) should come through the church account and a single check cut to the individual or group by the church.—Thus the church is aware of the total gifts, and each giver receives proper credit to his account.

8. The IRS now requires certification that none of the funds reported as contributions are for services rendered.—Stamps denoting "Restricted Account–Not for Contribution Credit" can be used for checks received by the church where value is received, such as church supper funds, T-Shirts, and camp fees. If the church is to keep the contribution credit now allowed by the IRS, the church must be careful to conform strictly with IRS regulations. Canceled checks, according to the IRS, are no longer proof of contributions; the giver must have a statement from the church.

Adapted from "Suggestions for the Budget and Finance Committee," *Stewardship Journal,* Winter 1997-98, 26.

72. (HOW TO) Develop a Ministry Budget for Your Church

Every church needs a plan for using the resources God has provided them. Here is a simple, step-by-step process that may be helpful. Gather the budget planning team about three months before the budget is to be adopted by the church.

Pray.—It's more than just a formality. Ask God to lead and bless in this important process. Consider asking those who will develop the budget to make a commitment to pray daily about the task before them. As stewards of God's resources, seek His will about how to use them.

Consider the purpose of your church.—This is an important, foundational step. Don't dismiss it or take a shortcut around it. How you spend the Lord's money has to be strongly linked to why your church exists. If your church has a formal purpose statement, review it at this time. If your church does not have a purpose statement, consider developing one. If your church is hesitant to enter this process, at least lead the committee to discuss why God has planted a church in that place.

Gather Information.
• Look at past budgets. What spending priorities are revealed in these budgets? Are ministries or items absent which should be included. Consider items purchased "outside the budget." Could some of these things have been anticipated in a well-planned budget?
• Consider giving patterns. In most churches, it is possible to anticipate the giving level per attendee. If, for example, your giving has averaged $20 per person in average Sunday School attendance, that will likely be the case during the coming year. If more dollars are required to provide needed ministries, it is then possible to plan growth that will provide those financial resources. Considering giving patterns is a valid, spiritual endeavor. It is wise stewardship.
• Consider possible ministries that will need funding during the coming year. What ministries were done in the past? What ministries should have been done? One way to approach this study of possible ministries is to use the five functions of the church as a guide.[1] Every church

should be busy doing five things–evangelism, discipleship, fellowship, ministry, and worship. Consider possible ministries under each of these functions.

• Look at growth (or decline) patterns of your church. If your church is growing, that pattern will probably continue. If your church is plateaued or declining, it will probably require intentional planning to reverse that trend.

• The level of fellowship or oneness is a valid consideration at budget planning time. The presence of a serious schism in the fellowship of your church may suggest that dramatic increases in the budget are unwise.

Gather budget input from the leadership team.[2]–Invite each person who leads an organization or is responsible for a ministry to submit proposals. These people represent the church on mission. Do all you can to enable the church to do all the ministries proposed.

Develop the Ministry Action Budget.–Consider including the following ministries.

• Our Mission Ministries
• Our Pastoral Ministries
• Our Christian Education Ministries
• Our Music Ministries
• Our Supportive Ministries
• Our Building and Grounds Ministries

Be sure to state all budget items as ministries. Even your building maintenance is done to facilitate ministry.

Present the Ministry Action Budget to the church for adoption.–Use visitation, direct mail, audiovisual presentations, a budget fair, panel discussions, and worship service presentations to tell the church about the proposed budget.

---

[1]Gene Mims, *Kingdom Principles for Church Growth*, revised and expanded (Nashville: LifeWay Press, 2001).

[2]*ABC's of Church Budgeting and Promotion* (ISBN 0-7673-240-X) contains a good Ministry Project Proposal form as well as more detail about this process.

73. (HOW TO) Manage Conflict in a Church

Conflict is universal and a natural part of life where people and relationships are involved. Understanding the difference between inner, interpersonal, and organizational conflict and separating people from organizational issues is vital.

Principles

1. Inner conflict without resolution can act out in different ways. This can affect family relationships and job performance as well as attitude in ministering and witnessing.
2. Dealing effectively with conflicts involving interpersonal relationships requires moving beyond immediate tensions and disagreements and identifying the root causes.
3. Miscommunication or lack of communication is often the root cause of most disagreements. Getting the parties to talk may resolve the conflict or misunderstanding.
4. If the conflict is deeper than mere communication, a neutral, third party may be needed to assist in negotiating resolution. This person can help identify issues, find common ground, and deal with deeper issues.
5. In dealing with organizational conflict, the issues need to be identified before resolution can begin to take place. Both hidden and surface issues must be addressed.

Approaches

Avoiding.—Sometimes the best approach is to ignore the situation. Some situations are best left alone. Even if you are right, you often lose. The battle may simply not be worth the cost. Getting involved will sometimes escalate the disagreement into a major conflict. Learn when it is best to walk away.

Avoiding blaming.—"Blamestorming" is a popular sport today. Pointing a finger and placing blame on others is easy. More difficult is extending one's hand in a move toward reconciliation.

153

Accommodating.—Hoping to preserve a relationship at all costs, some people automatically give in to the wishes of others. This is appropriate when the issues are unimportant compared to the value of the relationship or when the accommodating person feels that he or she is in the wrong. In other instances accommodating may give others a sense of vindication, even when they are wrong, which might lead to further conflict. The relationship may begin to feel burdensome, which can result in feelings of frustration and resentment. After repeated accommodations and continued conflict, another approach is needed.

Compromising.—Sometimes issues are too complex for involved parties to resolve. A mediator can help those involved to bring issues to the surface, while being sensitive to feelings involved. The goal is to have the parties work together to find mutually satisfactory solutions.

Negotiating.—The situation may necessitate bringing in a neutral, third party to help adversaries work through the issues. The tension level may be too high for the parties to talk without strong emotions. The neutral party can listen, help them talk through the issues, and help them become aware of ways to resolve the conflict.

Forcing.—After listening to the issues and working past any form of resolution, a mediator seeks to explore all possible solutions. The mediator has no power to impose them on the conflicting parties. Those in disagreement can be asked to accept a solution and to agree to work together.

Paul said that love is the greatest gift (see 1 Cor. 13). Ultimately the best solutions to any conflict are love and forgiveness.

Adapted from Richard Faling, "Managing Conflict Before It Manages You," *Church Administration*, November 1996, 10-12.

74. (HOW TO) Initiate Healthy Change in the Church

Every living thing is in the process of change. Every living church is in the process of change. In fact, change is essential to both life and health. Even churches that resist change are changing. While we cannot eliminate change, we can direct and manage change. The changes that come to our church should be planned and intentional.

The first step to initiating healthy change in a church is to understand some reasons people resist change. In *Pastoral Leadership for Growing Churches*, Bruce Grubbs pointed out some reasons people resist change.

- Because it threatens their sense of security.
- Out of reverence for and preservation of that which has grown "holy."
- Because they are afraid to risk.
- When it represents a loss of control.
- Because of pride—"Change is good—if it is my idea."
- When it affects their identity.[1]

Here is a process that may help you bring healthy change in your church.

Learn About Change
During this phase, the leader should learn about the process. Attend a conference, read a book or article, etc. This step is not just to learn about the change under consideration but also to learn about change in general.

Earn the Right to Propose Change
Be an effective, trusted leader before attempting to initiate significant change. Earn the right by proving yourself trustworthy, staying a while, doing your homework.

Make a Commitment to the Proposed Change
At this point in the process, it is usually not wise to make this commitment irrevocable. Make a commitment, but realize that not every fight is one you are willing to die for. Sometimes we need to back off a while and wait for a

better time. Realize, however, that some level of commitment is required because all change will face opposition.

Create Change Agents
Every involved person will be either an agent of change or a resistor to change. A change agent understands why the change is needed and how the change will come about. Invest your energy in creating agents of change. A conversation over a cup of coffee may accomplish more than a slick presentation during a business meeting.

Involve Many People
Invite those impacted by the change to participate in the change process from the early stages. They may have good and helpful insights. Be sure to involve those most impacted by the change.

Communicate the Change
Get the word out. It is probably a mistake to surprise a congregation with significant change. Let them know what is coming and why.

Formalize and Celebrate
Bring a sense of completion to the change process. If you begin a new Bible study group, have them stand and brag on them. If you change the order of worship, pause after about a month, and celebrate the warmth and spontaneity created by the change.

Remember, Jesus initiated more change than anyone in history.

---

[1]Bruce Grubbs, *Pastoral Leadership for Growing Churches* (Nashville: Convention Press, 1988), 55–57.

75. (HOW TO) Respond to an Offending Brother or Sister

1. Recognize that human conflict, in or out of the church, usually stems from tensions created when the interests of one person or group are positioned against the interests of another (see Phil. 4:2-3; Acts 15:1-35).

2. Remember and communicate that the personal rights of a Christian often must be subordinated, in the interests of a positive Christian witness and the good of other persons (see Matt. 5:38-42; 26:52; Rom. 12:11-21; 1 Cor. 13:4-7; Phil. 2:3-4). Related to this point is another principle: There is a difference between standing for personal rights and in standing for what is right (see 1 Cor. 8:13; 10:23-24, 31; Phil. 3:4-7).

3. Be sensitive to what is the right attitude and action in conflict situa-tions and to its dependence on Christian maturity as expressed in:
   • Putting the interests of others above personal interests.
   • Openness and eagerness to follow the Holy Spirit's leadership (see John 14:26; 16:12-13; 1 Cor. 2:6-13; Phil 2:3-4; 1 John 2:26-27).

4. Go to the New Testament for at least four models on how to deal with fellowship problems in the church:
   (1) If you have offended a brother, Matthew 5:23-26 indicates the following:
      • Your worship is hindered by a broken relationship.
      • Stop what you are doing and be reconciled with your brother.
      • After reconciliation, you and your offering then are more acceptable to God.
      • Reconciliation is to be sought quickly and privately.
   (2) If a brother has offended you, Matthew 18:15-22 specifies:
      • You are to go personally and try to be reconciled with your brother. Regardless of who the offender is, each believer is responsible for seeking reconciliation.
      • If you are not heard or are rebuffed, you are to take others with you as a witness to your desire for reconciliation.

- If the group is not heard or is rebuffed, you are to ask for church support.
- If the offending brother continues to refuse reconciliation, you have fulfilled your Christian duty.
- But the reconciliation process is to be pursued in patience and forgiveness and over a period of time dictated by love, not the stated limits of church policy or law.

(3) If two unreconciled brothers go to court to settle their dispute, 1 Corinthians 6:1-13 indicates the following:
- To take such an action is a negative reflection upon the rest of the church.
- To pursue legal action is to turn over to public courts problems the church should resolve.
- Both parties should rather be wronged or defrauded than to subject themselves and the church to this negative witness to the world.
- To take such action is to deny the spiritual life that each party has in Christ.

(4) If two sisters have a disagreement, Philippians 4:2-23 points out these principles:
- Reconciliation is vitally important to them and the church.
- The church is not to be passive, but active, in seeking reconciliation.
- The blessings of past happy relationships are not to be forgotten.

5. Will these principles work in the contemporary church? They will, if:
- There is a genuine, Spirit-induced, personal and congregational burden for reconciliation.
- Actions are taken in genuine Christian love.
- Ego, pride, and personal rights are subordinated to the good of the other party and the body as a whole.
- There is a broad base of personal and congregational openness to the transforming leadership of the Holy Spirit.
- The church genuinely wants to be the body of Christ, instead of merely a religious organization.

Adapted from Earl Waldrup, "How to Reclaim an Offending Brother," *Great Commission Breakthrough: "How to" Ideas for Great Commission Churches* (Nashville: The Sunday School Board of the Southern Baptist Convention, 1992), 34.

76. (HOW TO) Lead Deacons to Be Involved in Ministry

Deacons can provide much of the care that is needed by a congregation. The very word *deacon* points to service to persons in need.

Qualities Needed by Caring Deacons
- A caregiver knows Jesus Christ.
- A caregiver is sensitive.
- A caregiver is selfless.
- A caregiver is patient.
- A caregiver is alert.
- A caregiver gets involved.
- A caregiver is teachable.
- A caregiver grows spiritually.

Opportunities for Giving

The following listing is only representative of the many needs that exist in most churches. Your deacon group might compile its own list.

Assimilating new church members.
- Be willing to become personally involved.
- Assign specific responsibilities. If your deacon group wants to minister to new church members, an approach can be developed of assigning a deacon to each new member.

Helping newcomers to the community.—Your deacon group could find ways to reach out to newcomers to your community. Newcomers need to know where to find various support systems needed to carry on daily life. This support system includes doctors, attorneys, schools, shopping, recreation, and repair shops.

Caring for the pastor, church staff, and their families.—Who meets the emotional and physical needs of those in your church who serve the Lord vocationally?
- Provide encouraging words and helping hands.
- Encourage your church personnel committee to meet at least twice a year with the pastor and staff to evaluate salaries, time off, and work expectations.

- When a mistake is made by the pastor or a staff minister, encourage the congregation to deal with the mistake by following the guidelines given in Matthew 18:21-35 and Galatians 6:1-10.
- Encourage the pastor and staff to take time off weekly.
- Pray daily and at each deacons meeting for a strong level of trust to develop among pastor, staff, and deacons.
- Covenant together as deacons and fellow ministers to have a relationship of love, trust, and support for one another and to the work God has called you in Christ.

Providing for benevolence needs.—Performing acts of benevolence in the name of Christ aligns today's deacons with their counterparts in the New Testament church.

- Be alert to spot benevolent needs when visiting in homes.
- Develop guidelines to follow for the benevolent ministry.
- Investigate all requests. Obtain information regarding needs, eligibility, and amount of assistance required.
- Determine available help from community agencies. Sometimes certain kinds of long-term help can be given by such agencies. Have available a list of these agencies and the kind of assistance they can provide.
- Review periodically all assistance being provided.
- Make monthly reports to the deacon group regarding assistance given.

Ministering to specific need groups.—Singles, teens, students, the mentally retarded, hearing-impaired persons, nursing-home residents, and shut-ins are examples of special need groups.

Providing care in times of crisis.—At one time or another, the crises of sickness, bereavement, estrangement, or loneliness trouble most folks in the church family. Your ministry does not replace the pastor's ministry but enables the pastor to spend more time with the individuals who have the greatest needs.

Ministering to the needs of families.—Deacons are the natural group to provide care for families in the church through:

- Encouraging family worship.
- Shepherding new families into the fellowship of the church.
- Witnessing to families.
- Meeting special family needs such as homes broken by separation and divorce, problems with children, aged parents, substance abuse, physical abuse, crisis counseling, premarital pregnancy.
- Discovering families in need.
- Alerting the Church Council of general family needs.
- Maintaining a relationship between the church and community agencies.

77. (HOW TO) Lead Your Church to Elect Qualified Deacons

Churches have adopted many ways of electing deacons. Any method used by a church should reflect its polity, scriptural qualifications, and a commitment to ministry.

Deacon Nominations

Deacons serve the church, therefore the entire church should be given an opportunity to nominate persons to be elected and ordained as deacons. Each church member is asked to nominate one or more persons to be considered for election. These nominations would be made from a list showing deacons already ordained but not actively serving, church members who served as deacon in previous churches, and persons not previously ordained as deacons.

Deacon Nominating Committee

Prior to the time church members begin to nominate one or more persons for consideration as deacon, a deacon nominating committee should be appointed. This committee could be made up of five to seven people representative of the congregation. The deacon nominating committee members should be chosen in the same way regular church committee members are chosen. What is discouraged is using a committee made up only of deacons. Deacons are not a self-perpetuating body and never should give the appearance of being so.

The nominations from the church come to the deacon nominating committee. This committee will know how many deacons are needed in this particular election. This committee will conduct its work according to the church's policies. Matters such as age, length of church membership, whether already a deacon, a deacon having previously served as deacon in another church will be considered relative to each person nominated from the congregation. When considering the names nominated by the church, the deacon nominating committee should consider the names according to the number of nominations a person received.

Deacon Election

The deacon nominating committee presents to the church for election the same number of people that are needed. If five deacons are needed, then only five people are presented to the congregation for election.

Why use this suggested process or a similar one?

1. This process avoids embarrassing runoffs.
2. This process prevents some deacons from being elected by an embarrassingly small number of votes.
3. This process can help prevent the church's electing individuals who are not qualified.
4. This process helps potential deacons to understand the church's expectations for its deacons.

What might be described as the "absolutely best way" for all churches to elect deacons does not exist. The best way is what works most effectively for the church. Whatever method is used church members should be informed about the procedures for electing deacons, as well as the church's qualifications and duties of deacons. The election of deacons should be a meaningful experience that strengthens the fellowship of the church.

Resources

The Deacon—a quarterly magazine published by LifeWay Church Resources. To order call 1-800-458-2772.

Webb, Henry. *Deacons Servant Models in the Church,* updated edition. Nashville: Broadman & Holman, 2001.

78. (HOW TO) Ordain Deacons

The word *ordination* means "to select or appoint." A service of ordination expresses the church's confidence in the person being ordained. The church is saying, "We affirm your spiritual qualities, your devotion to God, your commitment to the church, and your potential for servant ministry."

The ordination service should be planned well so it becomes a memorable hour of worship and celebration. It should be meaningful for those ordained and their families.

Time of the Ordination Service

Conduct the ordination service prior to the elected deacons' period of service. For example, if the deacons begin their service on October 1, have the ordination service in September.

Participants in the Ordination Service

Who will actually lay hands on the deacons to be ordained? Today many churches ask that all members participate in the laying on of hands. This action emphasizes that deacons are servants of the whole church. Other churches ask only ordained persons to lay on hands. An explanation of the laying on of hands should be given to the congregation. Your church may choose to have a deacon installation service in addition to the ordination service. This would give the church an opportunity to affirm the deacons who will serve but were ordained at some previous time.

The Ordination Council

The ordination council provides a time to question and examine each candidate. The questions should be asked by a gathering of ordained men and should include the personal testimony of the candidate. The candidate should also express his understanding of the servant role of deacons and his commitment to service. After the council has completed its work and is satisfied that the candidate is worthy of ordination, the council should bring a formal recommendation to the church that the church proceed with the intended ordination service. Many churches choose to have the meeting of the ordination council immediately before the ordination service. While this is convenient for those participating, it leaves open the possibility that unforeseen and unexpected events will embarrass the church or the candidates. The meeting of the ordination council should probably take place at least one week prior to the ordination service. This timing allows the questioning of ordination candidates to be meaningful and lessens the possibility that the ordination council will ordain someone who is not acceptable to the church or the Lord.

The Ordination Service

The order of worship will vary according to local church practice and tradition, but here are a few things you probably will want to consider.

- Music and Scripture readings should be chosen to fit the theme of the service.
- Appropriate responsive readings could be used.
- The pastor should give an explanation of the purpose of the service.
- Married deacon candidates could sit with their wives on the front row of pews.
- Testimonies by the deacon candidates should be arranged well in advance of the ordination service. Wives may wish to stand beside their husbands during these testimonies.
- The charge to the deacons should be given to the deacon candidates by a respected deacon or pastor. This person may be from your church or another church.
- A reception for the newly ordained deacons should follow the service.
- Present a certificate or gift to the newly ordained deacons.

The ordination service should be a time of prayer, worship, and commitment to Christ and the work of His church. This occasion can be an encouragement to all the deacons as the church assures them of the church's acceptance and support.

Adapted from Bob Sheffield, "A Deacon Ordination Service," *Church Administration*, December 1989, 10-11.

79. (HOW TO) Involve Deacons in Benevolent Ministry

Most New Testament churches are involved in benevolent ministries. Depending on the church's location, this type ministry can make a real difference in the community and can go far in meeting the needs of residents and passersby. It can also be time-consuming.

Involving deacons in the church's benevolent ministry gives deacons an opportunity to minister, allows deacons to exercise their unique gifts in ministry, encourages them to lead others to get involved, and gives time back to the pastor for other ministry opportunities.

Acts 6 set the pattern for laymen in the church to meet the needs of members. Today's deacons can follow this example.

1. Deacons with a family ministry plan can use this organization as the basic approach to meet the needs of church families.

2. Deacons can take the lead in establishing a church plan for a benevolent ministry to help meet the needs of nonmembers in the church community.

3. The first step in beginning a benevolent ministry should be a study of relevant Scriptures. Include such passages as Acts 6, Matthew 25:35-40. Deacons may elect to study a book designed for this purpose. Contact the North American Mission Board for current titles. Such a study will help deacons identify those whom God is leading to participate in this ministry.

4. One or two of the leaders in the benevolent ministry should make plans to discover what other agencies in the community are doing and how the church can work alongside those groups. This partnership will help eliminate duplication and fraud and will improve the assistance rendered those in need.

5. The next step in beginning a benevolent ministry is to determine who may receive the benefits (members and/or nonmembers), assess needs,

consider resources available, and select the kinds of ministries to be offered.

6. After deacons have determined needs and direction, they should let the church family know of their plans. Others will want to help when they hear about the needs deacons have discovered and the opportunities to help meet those needs.

7. Confidentiality is also a significant element of benevolent ministry. This is especially true when meeting the needs of church members and nonmembers in small towns or communities.

8. Monthly reports to the church will keep members aware and interested. Make the reports as personal as possible without betraying confidences. Just telling numbers of people served or money spent will not draw new volunteers. Let those who have helped in the benevolent ministry share the joy of service.

A benevolent ministry is a wonderful way to join God at work in your community.

Adapted from Bob Patterson, "Deacons and Benevolence Ministry," *The Deacon*, Summer 1997, 14-15.

Resource

Henry, Jim. *Deacons: Partners in Ministry and Growth Kit*. Distributed by LifeWay Church Resources.

80. (HOW TO) Develop an Effective 12-Month Outreach Plan

Three simple, yet intentional steps will enhance the outreach ministry of any church.

1. Train your people in outreach.—At least twice a year, train your people in outreach. Excellent witness training resources can be found in *Outreach Teams That Win: G.R.O.W.* by Jerry Tidwell. This resource also contains help for training your people to make a visit. Other resources are *Share Jesus Without Fear*, and FAITH—a resource for doing evangelism through the Sunday School. The next article in this resource, "How to Train People in Evangelism," also contains some helpful ideas.

2. Plan and conduct four prospect discovery projects each year.—Once a quarter, do something intentional about finding prospects. Your total number of prospects should be approximately equal to your Sunday School enrollment.
- Register people who attend church activities and ministries, and get as much accurate information as possible.
- Do a bulk mail project targeted to some community near your church. Determine the demographic profile of those in the community. What would they respond to? If it is a community of young adults, perhaps they would like an audiotape of a Christian counselor talking about discipline in the home or how to prepare their preschooler for school. If the community is filled with senior adults, they might be more interested in information about maintaining health and happiness during retirement. Use the mailed brochure to offer the gift to those who return the post-paid response card or call the given number. Be sure the brochure is professional in appearance.
- Conduct a prayer needs search. Instead of a traditional door-to-door survey, enlist a team of prayer warriors. Go door-to-door telling people about your new prayer ministry. Ask if they would like the prayer team to pray for them. Record the information, and pray for a week. Then return to the prospect to see how they are doing. Caution: Really minister to them. Don't just use prayer to find prospects.

- Have a bicycle safety demonstration for children in the neighborhood. Ask the local police department to provide a safety presentation.
- Constantly search for new prospect discovery ideas. Talk with other pastors, attend conferences, buy books, pray. If you search and pray, you can find one good prospect discovery idea for every three months.

3. Plan and conduct four outreach participation events each year.
- Establish an outreach center. Using a table or bulletin board, make outreach assignments available after Sunday School and worship. Place the center in a high-traffic area. Someone who is familiar with the prospect file should be there to help with assignments.
- Have a pie night. Ask members to make pies and deliver them to absentees. Offer to pray for them or take prayer requests back to the pastor.
- Have a Team Reach Month. Announce that during Team Reach there will be several different ways for people to participate in outreach. Set up an outreach room with several kinds of well-labeled outreach possibilities. Include Evangelism, Absentee, Ministry, Newcomer, and Hospital visits. Also invite people to participate in outreach by staying at the church to pray, make phone calls, or write cards or letters.
- Conduct a literature visitation project. Purchase some piece of literature for every member of your Sunday School. Label literature so that every member's name is on a piece. Ask teachers to deliver literature to the home of each member. If teachers cannot deliver all the literature, enlist others to help. Remember, the purpose of literature visitation is not to distribute literature. It is to visit every member of the Sunday School.

Resources
Tidwell, Jerry. *Outreach Teams That Win: G.R.O.W.* Nashville: Convention Press, 1997.

Fay, William. *Share Jesus Without Fear.* Nashville: LifeWay Press, 1997.

FAITH (a resource for doing evangelism through the Sunday School). For more information call 1-800-254-2022.

81. (HOW TO) Establish a Prospect File

In the fall of 1993, as I began a new ministry through the Sunday School
Board (now LifeWay Christian Resources), my family and I had a new
experience. We prayerfully chose a new church home. You see, my father
was a pastor, my wife's father was a pastor, and I had served as a pastor
for more than 18 years. The only way we had chosen a church was in
the context of determining where God would have us provide pastoral
leadership. When we found the community where we would live, we visited
three churches. Each one came to our home, and we enjoyed all the visits.
One of the three did something that really set them apart from the others.

The woman from the church knocked on the door. When we opened
the door, she introduced herself and said: "It was good to have you in
our services last Sunday. I am a teacher in Preschool Sunday School, and
I wonder if I might spend a few minutes with your daughter, Katie." She
spent the next 10 minutes with my daughter. She told Katie about the Bible
story for next week. She told her who would sit with her and what games
they would play.

When the teacher left, my preschooler felt like the most important
person in the world. She said, "Daddy, she came to see me."

The next day a worker from one of the children's classes called my son
and spent a few minutes on the phone with him. Guess what? We went to
that church the next week. In fact, we never visited another church. We
joined in a few weeks.

This effective outreach was made possible because the church had a
useable prospect file. In fact, these contacts would probably not have been
made if Katie had been a note on my prospect card. The church had a
separate card for each member of my family.

Establish a prospect file. The master file should include each family of
prospects. Be sure to get as much information as possible. In addition to
the master file, use the pocket and card system as a working file. This system
is designed to be kept in notebooks. In the smaller church, or the church
with few prospects, begin with four notebooks. Use one notebook for
preschoolers, another for children, one for youth, and one for adults. Even
if some of these notebooks will be empty when you begin, label one for
each age group. Ultimately, you will want one notebook for each class or
department, but begin with one per age group.

Now you are ready to fill your prospect file. Be patient. A steady flow of new prospects is better than finding hundreds all at once. Schedule one prospect discovery project for each quarter of the year. Be consistent in getting complete information on anyone who participates in activities or ministries of your church. Remember to ask church members for names and addresses of people they know who need Bible study.

Note: Many churches use computers to manage prospect information. If you choose this approach, be aware of these factors.

- The prospect assignment card or sheet you print out should be easy to assign. Giving a Sunday School teacher a sheet with 10 prospects on it means the teacher would have to cut it into strips to make an outreach assignment in class. Most teachers won't do this.
- The prospect assignment card or sheet you print out should be designed with the expectation that it will be returned with a report of the visit. Accountability is essential.

82. (HOW TO) Get Names and Information from People Who Visit Your Services

It happens hundreds of times every week. The guest family arrives just as the choir is singing the call to worship. They slip in the back door and sit on the back row. They leave quickly after (or sometimes during) the benediction, giving you and your congregation almost no opportunity even to say hello. Then they sometimes complain that your church isn't friendly.

How do you follow up on that prospect? In an age when many people desire anonymity, how do we get names, addresses, and phone numbers from people like these?

The basic principle is simple. Your guests are more likely to do what everyone else in the congregation is doing. If everyone fills out a card, they will likely fill out a card. If everyone else tears a tab off the bulletin, they will likely do the same. Therefore, I am convinced that the best approach is a bulletin with a tear-off response tab. Next best choice is a guest registration card in the pew rack.

1. During the welcome time, ask everyone to tear off the tab all at once. The person welcoming the guests should have a bulletin in hand and tear off the tab before the people.

2. Invite all the people in the congregation, including guests, to tear off and fill out the response tab.

3. Emphasize communicating prayer needs with the response tab. This will encourage regular attendees to fill out the tab and communicate vital prayer concerns as well. The Church Bulletin Service Response Bulletins with response tabs include a place for prayer concerns. If you print your own bulletins, be sure to include this feature.

4. Reinforce the need for regular attendees to tear off and fill out the response tab each week. The smaller the church, the more difficult it will be to get your people to do this. On occasional Sunday nights, talk with your people about the importance of everyone filling out

the response tab. Remind them that guests are much more likely to give you the information you need if everyone fills out the card. Encourage them to communicate prayer concerns through this method.

5. Some people simply will not fill out a response tab. Establish a welcome center and encourage the welcome center team to get as much information as possible.

6. Enlist a few friendly people to make their way to the exits during the benediction. Train them to speak to guests and make them feel welcome. In the process, ask this team to get as much information as possible.

7. The smaller membership church is the most difficult place to establish good welcome procedures and keep them going. The reason it is more difficult in the smaller church is that these churches often go several weeks without a guest. It takes real discipline to be ready for guests every week, when you have guests only every fourth or fifth week. Be ready for guests every week. Keep those guest-welcoming processes in place even when several weeks pass without a guest.

Resources
Church Bulletin Service Response Bulletins. Produced by LifeWay Church Resources. For more information call 1-800-458-2772.

83. (HOW TO) Train People in Evangelism

How to share your faith is something every Christian should know. The Great Commission commands us to make disciples in every part of the world. Why, then, are so many Christians convinced that witnessing is so difficult? The answer is simple. Satan has deceived us. Christians have fallen for his tricks. Sharing your faith ought to be simple. In fact, if your experience with Jesus is genuine, telling someone about it is natural. Remember, the Lord has never commanded you to be like anyone else. Your testimony is your story. Witnessing is as simple as telling someone else about that which you have experienced yourself.

When I was 16 years old, in 1968, my dad helped me buy an old car. It took me nine months to pay the $300 price of the car. But to me, that car was just about the greatest thing in my life. You know what I did? I did something very natural and easy. I told all my friends (and most of my acquaintances) about my new car. I didn't need a training class. I didn't worry if someone would ask me hard car questions. I just talked about my car all the time because I was excited about my car. A similar excitement about Jesus should result in a natural witness about Him.

I appreciate the value of witness training classes. I know that many people need help developing a personal testimony that communicates with lost people. We sometimes complicate what should be a simple thing.

One witness training approach I have found helpful is built around two questions. The discussion around these questions provides an opportunity to deepen believers' understanding of exactly what happened to them when they were saved. It also provides an opportunity for participants to develop a personalized witnessing approach that describes, in words easily understood, a person's new birth experience.

What Must a Person Know to Be Saved?

In most of the places I have asked this question, the discussion has produced a rather long list of answers. Some have suggested that you must know the Bible to be saved. Others say one must "really understand the meaning of forgiveness." Soon the list begins to seem unrealistic. Someone may say, "I didn't know much about the Bible when I was saved," or, "I'm not sure I fully understand forgiveness now."

When it becomes clear that the list is much too long, ask the second

question and lead the group in a brief discussion of the few things one must really know to be saved. Although this article is not intended to be an exhaustive theological study, your short list should certainly include the following.
- You must know you have sinned.
- You must know who Jesus is.
- You must know how to receive Him as your personal Lord and Savior.

What Must a Person Do to Be Saved?

In discussing this question, the trainees will be more careful what they put on the list. Insist that they use language a lost person could understand. Also make a distinction between actions that bring salvation and those that follow salvation. For example, someone will probably suggest that one must walk the aisle or be baptized to be saved. These are actions that come before or after salvation, but they do not answer the question, What must a person do to be saved?

Ask a few people to share what they did when they were saved. Trainees may find it difficult to articulate the actions they took in receiving Christ. Gently insist that they identify those actions and put them in words a lost person could understand. If, for example, they say, "I gave my heart to Jesus," ask: "What does that mean? What did you do when you gave your heart to Jesus?"

Somewhere along the way, every person who has experienced new birth has talked to God. That prayer included a confession of sin, a request for forgiveness, repentance, and an invitation for Jesus to enter that person's life. Continue to probe gently until trainees can articulate their own conversion. Be prepared to share your own new birth experience in words a lost person could understand.

After a thorough discussion of what a person must do to be saved, invite participants to practice telling their own conversion stories to each other. Partners can help eliminate words and terms lost and unchurched people would not understand.

Witnessing is as natural as telling your friends about your new car. Discussing these two questions can help Christians articulate their testimony.

174

84. (HOW TO) Plan Effective Revivals

Revivals have played such an important part in the life of our country and in most of our lives that churches should make the revival meeting a priority. What steps are necessary to prepare for a successful revival? Salvation is of the Lord, and real revival comes from God; however, some steps are necessary to implement an effective revival meeting.

Planning

(Prayer is really first, but we'll deal with that later.)
• Establish the date for the meeting. Avoid calendar conflicts.
• Determine how long the revival will last. In the past, two-week revivals were common. Now three days is more common. The pastor should lead his people to have as long a revival meeting as possible.
• Decide the kind of revival your church needs. Does your church need spiritual renewal or an evangelistic harvest? What about an emphasis on the home or a Sunday School revival?

People

One of the keys to successful revival is the selection of persons who will lead the meeting. The leadership of the Holy Spirit in selecting the preacher is absolutely essential.

Consider inviting a full-time evangelist at least once a year. We should recognize that God has called some to be evangelists and use them in our churches. Many times it is also wise to invite a music evangelist or minister of music to lead the revival music.

Program

What will be the features of the revival? What are some ways to get people to attend?

Special-night emphases can help. Some special-night emphases could be: Children's Night, Youth Night, Men's Night, Women's Night, Neighbor Night, Family Night, Sunday School Night, Deacon's Night, or Old-Fashioned Night.

Ask someone to serve as chairperson for that special night. Let those chairpersons enlist others to help them on their assigned nights. The more people involved in planning, the better the attendance.

Promotion
- Revival posters.
- Newspaper announcements.
- Church newsletter.
- Sunday School.
- Prayer in worship services.
- Word of mouth. (This is most effective for lost people.)
- Sow sparingly, reap sparingly. Sow bountifully, reap bountifully.

Prospects
- Prospects on the Sunday School roll.
- Husbands, wives, or children of church members.
- Your prospect file.
- Visitors cards from your worship services.

Prayer
Revival cannot happen apart from effective praying by God's people. Cottage prayer meetings are still effective. A leader should be enlisted for each home to bring a short devotion and begin the prayer time.

Offer special prayer times at the church for your people to drop by and pray during the week.

Praise
When God blesses, His people should acknowledge the blessing through praise.

Adapted from Billie Friel, "Planning Revival Services," *Church Administration*, October 1987, 17.

85. (HOW TO) Make a Visit

Outreach Teams That Win: G.R.O.W. is one of the finest outreach resources to be found. In it, author Jerry Tidwell provides some excellent tips on how to make a visit.

Set the time to go.–The ministry of visitation, if not planned, usually never happens.

Don't be pushy.–Leave the door open for future visits. Ask the person if he or she would allow you to come inside for a brief time of discussion about your church. Allow the prospect to make that decision.

Don't embarrass the prospect.–Generally, if the prospect is embarrassed by your conversation, you have not handled it properly.

Understand the principle of harvest.–Harvest will not come unless sowing and cultivation come first. The harvest may come several weeks after the initial visit.

Be clean and neat.–Dress casually. Let your dress communicate that the visit is important but not formal.

Go "two by two."–Follow the example of Jesus in Luke 10:1. Certain circumstances of the visit are more easily handled when two are present.

Be courteous.–If the prospect has company or is in the middle of dinner, the visitation team should graciously agree to come another time.

Don't be surprised by non-Christian behavior.–Remember, a change of heart will result in a change of behavior. Don't expect the change of behavior to occur first.

Avoid verbal overkill. Don't use language the prospect won't understand.

Be complimentary.–Find something about the person, the home, or the children that you can honestly compliment.

Know names and family information.—Never carry the prospect assignment card to the door. Become familiar with it before you approach the home.

Decide who will lead.—One person on the visitation team should lead the conversation.

Go to the front door.—Don't assume the prospect will expect guests at the back door.

Pray for the person you are visiting.—Before leaving the parking lot at the church, pause and pray for the visitation encounter.

Prepare introductory remarks.—Without sounding as if the remarks are canned, state your name, your partner's name, and the church you represent.

Show genuine interest in the prospect.—You cannot convey genuine interest without listening to the prospect.

Have a conversation plan.—Use the acrostic FORM.
> **F**   stands for questions about the *family.*
> **O**   represents conversation about *occupation* or work.
> **R**   is for the prospect's involvement in *religion* or church.
> **M**   stands for your *message* or the reason for your visit.

If the visit is to a person who has a saving relationship with Jesus, focus on the church. Love your church and show genuine excitement about it.

If the visit is to an unsaved person, be sensitive to the leadership of the Holy Spirit. Ask for permission to share your personal testimony.

Resource
Tidwell, Jerry. *Outreach Teams That Win: G.R.O.W.* Nashville: Convention Press, 1997.

86. (HOW TO) Reach Your Goal on High-Attendance Day in Sunday School

A high-attendance day can provide a needed boost for your Bible study ministry. It can lead your people to focus together toward a common goal. A high-attendance day can bring a sense of excitement to your entire church.

Here is a simple process for using high attendance day to boost involvement and enthusiasm in your Sunday School.

1. Set a Date

This is important. Choose a time when the calendar is clear of other priority emphases. Avoid holidays. Some prefer to link with natural high-attendance times (like Easter), while others see the wisdom of attacking those traditionally low-attendance times like mid-winter or summer slump. It is really encouraging to have an all-time record high attendance in Sunday School in the middle of what would have been a summer slump. This approach also has the added benefit of an accompanying boost in activity and attendance before and after the event.

2. Set the Goal

Be careful. If the goal is too high, people will be frustrated and discouraged. If it is too low, they will not be challenged. A few more than ever before is usually a good idea. Participation is best if the entire leadership team, including teachers, sets the goal.

3. Six Weeks Before the Big Day, Publish the First Weekly Countdown Bulletin

This is a simple, brief newsletter for teachers and other leaders, probably filling only one side of a half sheet of paper. At the top, place the theme of the high-attendance day. For example, if your event is near Valentine's Day, you may consider "Put Your Heart in the Church Day" for your theme. Then list the actions leaders should take to prepare for the special day. Distribute a countdown bulletin each week until the event. Here are

a few examples of things that might go in a countdown bulletin.
- Lead your class in praying that God will use "Put Your Heart in the Church Day" to reach people for Christ and involve them in life-changing Bible study.
- Set the attendance goal for your class.
- Discuss ways your class can help publicize "Put Your Heart in the Church Day."

4. Three Weeks Before the High-Attendance Day, Send a Personal, Hand-written Invitation to All Sunday School Members and Prospects

Print names and addresses of all members and prospects in groups of 10. Place each list, consisting of 10 names and addresses, in a large envelope. Also place an instruction sheet, a sample letter, a pen, and 10 church envelopes in the packet. Place the packets, each containing everything needed to write 10 letters, on the Lord's Supper table. Enlist members to take the packets home and hand-write the letters. Remind them to hand address the envelopes and bring the completed packet back to the church the next Sunday. It is best to mail all packets at once from the church.

5. Two Weeks Prior to the High-Attendance Day, Contact All Members and Prospects by Telephone

Use a process similar to step 4, but in each packet place the names and phone numbers of 10 members and prospects and an instruction sheet to equip your people to make the personal phone calls.

6. The Week Before the High-Attendance Day, Schedule a Visitation Blitz

Have outreach blitz activities at least three times during the week—one during a weekday morning, one for a weekday night, and one on Saturday morning.

When the big day comes, celebrate the victory. Brag on all the classes and departments that meet their goals. Enjoy the day.

87. **HOW TO** Establish a Welcome Center

The purpose of a welcome center is to welcome visitors to the church facility in a warm, personable, caring way; to direct them to the appropriate Sunday School class/department; to obtain complete record information on the entire family; and to invite guests to enroll in Bible study the first time they attend.

1. Recognize that first impressions are important and are influenced by ease of parking, attractive landscaping, signs and directions, and the friendliness and helpfulness of church members. Evaluate current efforts in these areas, and express a desire to improve.

2. Recommend a greeter program as a key way of creating a positive first impression.

3. Recommend implementation of a greeter program, possibly through the Sunday School outreach-evangelism organization.

4. Establish a welcome center as part of the greeter program, according to these and other criteria:
   Select a site (or sites) that is easily accessible and visible from the place visitors will probably park.—If space is not available, greeters may move around within the facility and provide the same assistance.
   Obtain materials for the welcome center:
   • Pencils or pens.
   • Name tags.
   • Registration and/or enrollment forms.
   • One or more copies of a map of the church (with all rooms numbered).
   • Baby Schedule Cards (BBS 4380-09).
   • Luggage tags or other identification for diaper bags.
   • Brochure giving information about age groups/Bible study provisions/other programs in the church.
   Enlist workers for the greeter program:
   • Hosts/hostesses for the welcome center.
   • Curbside greeters (parking lot).
   • Escorts (from the welcome center to classes/departments).

181

Select friendly, outgoing people as workers. Choose from among singles and young, median, and senior adults, keeping a balance of male and female workers.
Train welcome center workers.

5. Enlist and train two types of greeters—curbside greeters, to meet people on the parking lots on Sunday mornings; and inside greeters, who welcome guests immediately inside the building. Consider providing umbrellas for curbside greeters to use in inclement weather.

6. Establish a procedure such as the following for Sunday mornings:
   • Curbside greeters—Welcome guests in the parking lot.
   • Curbside greeters—Guide guests directly to the welcome center for registration.
   • Welcome center workers—Fill out information form on all guests. Invite them to enroll in Bible study.
   • Escorts—Take children to their departments and introduce parents to at least one teacher. Start with youngest child first. Leave information with the teacher.
   • Escorts—After the children have been taken to their departments, guide parents to their proper class/department and introduce them to the department director or outreach-evangelism leader.
   • Department leader—If guests have not already been asked to enroll, invite them to do so.
   • Class/department outreach-evangelism leader—Assume responsibility for the newcomer in these ways: (1) Introduce the guest to the teacher and class members. (2) Assign a class member to serve as host to the guest during the entire Bible study time and, if possible, during the worship service.

7. Consider other special features, such as visitor parking spaces close to the building.

8. Begin the greeter program.

9. Evaluate the program and make improvements.

Adapted from Jerri Herring, "How to Establish a Greeter Program," *Great Commission Breakthrough: "How to" Ideas for Great Commission Churches* (Nashville: The Sunday School Board of the Southern Baptist Convention, 1992), 18.

88. (HOW TO) Organize Your Church into Outreach Teams That Win

In *Outreach Teams That Win: G.R.O.W.*, Jerry Tidwell identified five principles for outreach.

The Principle of Sowing and Reaping
This is God's principle, and it applies everywhere. From the garden to the farm you can be sure that nothing will come up if you plant nothing.

Matthew 13:54-58 tells of Jesus' going to a community where He did not do many miracles because the people did not believe. Is it possible that Jesus will pass through your church and do no mighty works because of your unbelief? We demonstrate our unbelief by planting no evangelistic seed. God will pass through this week. If we plant seed, He will send a harvest. We cannot know which seed will bear fruit. Our task is to plant in faith and believe that God will do His part by bringing the harvest.

The Principle of Every Member Involvement
Outreach should be a ministry in which every church member can participate. Yet many of the people in our churches feel that they cannot participate in traditional outreach. They do not feel qualified to share an evangelistic witness, and they feel that they cannot commit one additional night a week for the rest of their lives.

The Principle That Outreach Is Fun
It must have been fun to be one of the 12 apostles during Jesus' earthly ministry. When Jesus was transfigured on Mt. Tabor and Peter said, "Let's stay here and build three tabernacles," he was having fun. When Jesus fed the 5,000 and they picked up 12 baskets of leftovers, it was fun. It still is fun to be a believer.

It's fun to tell others about Jesus. The devil has deceived us into thinking that outreach is a not enjoyable. Think back to the times you have led people to faith in Jesus. It's fun to see them begin to understand the simplicity of the gospel. It's fun to see them relieved of the burden of guilt they have been carrying. It's fun to see them begin to grow in the Lord. Outreach and evangelism are fun.

The Principle That Quality Time Is Greater Than Quantity Time

Jerry Tidwell put these principles into practice in a church he led as pastor. He asked the people to commit to one night of outreach a week for the next year. About 10 percent of the people responded positively. He later asked the same people to commit to one night of outreach a month for a year. This time 65 percent of the people agreed. When the church was organized into four outreach teams, and each team was responsible for one night a month, many more people participated in outreach.

This approach lowers the time demand but significantly raises accountability. If participants commit one night a month to outreach and are absent, they are expected to make up that outreach night.

The Principle of Divine Appointment

God is dealing with the hearts of lost persons every day. Somewhere a willing witness will intersect the life of one of those convicted persons, and they will be saved. Our task is to listen to God and go where He sends us. When we do, some will believe and receive the new birth. Not every witness is a divine appointment, but as you go, some will be.

On the basis of these five principles, consider the following actions.

Organize your church into four G.R.O.W. outreach teams–one for each week of the month. The "G" team goes out on the first Tuesday; the "R" team goes out on the second Tuesday, and so forth.

Enlist G.R.O.W. captains to lead the teams.–The captains will enlist the people to join a team and attend the evangelism training. You will need about one captain for every 20 members.

Train team members in evangelism.–Use the material in *Outreach Teams That Win: G.R.O.W.* to train team members.

Resource

Tidwell, Jerry. *Outreach Teams That Win: G.R.O.W.* Nashville: Convention Press, 1997.

89. (HOW TO) Reclaim Chronic Absentees

Every church has absentees—Sunday School members or even church members who seldom or never attend. Even with the most effective preventative measures, some chronic absenteeism will continue. However, a reasoned approach to this problem can yield positive results. It is possible to reach out in love to these people and reclaim some of them for meaningful participation in Bible study and church membership.

Understand how they became inactive.—In *Going: One on One* Harry Piland identified a cycle showing how some absentees become chronic absentees.
1. Unfulfilled expectations.
2. Disappointment.
3. Lack of ministry.
4. Further disappointment.
5. Lack of ministry.
6. Absenteeism.
7. Drop out.

As you can see, intervention at early stages of this cycle can be productive. In fact, the earlier ministry and contact take place, the more effective it will likely be.

Some people become inactive or absent because of a spiritual problem. Attendance at Bible study or worship is an uncomfortable reminder of their spiritual problem. The problem, spiritual or otherwise, may be deep and difficult to deal with, or it may be simple to address. In either case, an early caring contact is much more likely to produce a positive result.

A strong, well-organized Sunday School class is a good place to start. A class with good records and persons responsible for caring ministries will respond more quickly and effectively

Pray for absentees.—Ask the Sunday School class to pray intentionally for absentees. They will certainly want to pray on Sunday morning, but some members will commit to pray daily for the absentee.

Start a new Bible study group or class.—It may be easier for the absentee to respond to a new class. Embarrassment will be lessened, and the natural excitement of something new will build enthusiasm.

Consider a four-week prayer/contact/visitation blitz.

Week 1.–Ask class members to pray daily for absentees. Be sure someone is praying for each absentee.

Week 2.–Ask class members to call all absentees. Again, be sure everyone is called.

Week 3.–Ask class members to send cards or letters to each absentee–hand-written only, please, and no preprinted address labels.

Week 4.–Ask class members to gather at the church for a meal or snack and visit all absentees.

Visit the absentees.

1. Keep the emphasis on prayer.–No one would appreciate an accusatory, negative visit. Almost anyone would appreciate a caring visit that asks, "Can I take any prayer concerns back to your Sunday School class?"
2. Take absentees a small gift, just to let them know you care.–A plate of cookies or a cake can smooth over that awkward moment when absentees realize that someone from the church is there, and they will have to talk about their absence. Say something like: "We were having some dessert down at the church, and we didn't want you to be left out."
3. Expect some anger from absentees.–They may feel that their church let them down in their time of need. And they may be right. Don't try to ignore that anger. Allow them to express it, and deal with it in a gracious manner.
4. Don't defend or criticize others.–You probably don't know enough about that situation to know what happened.
5. Ask what it would take for them to come back and participate, once again, in Bible study.
6. Affirm that they are persons of worth to the church and class.
7. Suggest attending another class if they would be more comfortable.

90. (HOW TO) Publish a Great Newsletter

The purpose of a church newsletter is to get people to read it! Designing a newsletter that captures members' attention long enough to read it will keep them informed about the church's valuable activities and ministries. The goal is to make the newsletter so inviting that members will take the time to read it immediately rather than put it aside.

Enhance Readability

Readability means the newsletter is easy to read. Several factors affect readability.

Type size.—Is it large enough for an older person to read without squinting? The smaller the type, the more copy will fit on the page; but the larger the type, the easier it is to read. Most books, magazines, newsletters, and newspapers are printed in 10–12-point type. Most computers today will allow the user to select the point size.

Type style.—Type with small lines on the ends of the letters is called serifed type (like the type you are reading). Type without those small lines is called sans serif. An example of a serifed typeface found on most computers is Times. An example of a common sans serif typeface is Helvetica. Most people experience less fatigue when reading a type with serifs. Type without serifs is often used for headlines. Avoid any typeface that is difficult to read. The type should look open and uncrowded.

Color.—Using different colors of ink can appear innovative and exciting, but they are more difficult to read than black or navy. Limit use of a second color ink to headlines or brief copy.

The same is true for paper. The more intense the color of paper, the more difficult the copy is to read. White paper always is best for readability. Other choices may be light grey, soft beige, or a light pastel.

Other trends in color are screens as a background for type. Screens are printed in a percentage of the intensity of the color. The higher the percentage the darker the color and the more difficult the the piece is to read.

Readability is also influenced by paragraph length, word choice, and layout. Paragraphs should be short with two to five sentences. Words should be short and common. No one wants to find a dictionary to read a newsletter. Sentences should also be short, averaging about 10 words per sentence.

White space invites the reader in. Copy that is too crowded is uninviting.
Use one typeface consistently. Another typeface might be used occasionally for an announcement, invitation, or some other short special feature; but most of the copy should be in one typeface.

Create Interest

Graphics.–Quality, contemporary clip art is available from a number of sources from print to software. Using clip art from one source will give a newsletter a more polished, consistent, professional appearance.

Logos or icons.–Many newsletters now use icons for standing columns. Icons are small graphic illustrations or symbols that help readers quickly locate items of interest such as the pastor's column or the prayer list.

Brevity.–Keep articles short. If long articles must occasionally be included, break up the copy with subheads.

People.–People like to read about people. Members want to know about others in the congregation. Remember that shut-ins and absentees also read newsletters. Information about people increases interest.

Tone.–Keep it positive. Newsletters don't have a captive audience. Most people won't read a lecture.

Reader response.–Include action words and opportunities for response such as invitations, response forms, or phone numbers to call–for Wednesday evening dinner, a youth retreat, or a parenting workshop.

The goal of the newsletter is communication. It is another tool to serve God's people.

Adapted from Tim Floyd, "Unleashing an Unbeatable Newsletter," *Church Administration*, July 1993, 36–37.

Resource

Gandy, Donna J. *Ministry Office QuickSource*. Nashville: Convention Press, 1998.

91. (HOW TO) Manage the Image of Your Church

Every church has an image. In fact, a church has a number of images. Long-term members may see it entirely different from the way the youth see it. And members of the community see it one way, while those on the inside see it another. Those who have received ministry from the church see it one way, while those who have left the church may see it another.

Church leaders and members can take steps to clarify a church's image and to project that image intentionally into all areas of the church and community.

Form a Task Force or a Committee

This group works with others in the church who directly impact a church's image—the worship committee, the publicity committee, and the property and space committee, for example. Their responsibilities include:

Seek expert help.—Communicate the needs and expectations of this group to the church family. Let them know the type persons needed. Look for people who have expertise in marketing, interior design, landscaping, advertising and promotion, writing, art, space management, and media.

Define their role.—Offer the group a job description, but let them further refine their role. Tasks might include:

- Identify public relations and image management needs.
- Determine priorities.
- Identify media that will best achieve priorities with the available budget.
- Develop a five-year and a detailed, dated, one-year, immediate-action plan.
- Make assignments within the committee. Implement the one-year action plan and other immediate actions.
- Educate the staff and other church committees about the work of this committee.
- Stay current on image development and media tools.
- Evaluate all actions and activities continually.

Clarify the vision.—Look at ideas that have arisen; determine if the ideas are within the scope of this group; and seek creative ways to involve more people.

Intentionally Establish Identity

Few churches can be all things to all people. Most churches don't have enough budget and buildings to meet every need in the community. Churches must be intentional about establishing an identity in the communities they serve.

Seek a definite strategy.–What images come to mind when the committee thinks about the church? Which of these best describes the church?

Take advantage of primary and secondary data.–Primary data is gathered by the committee. It includes interviews, canvassing, and opinion surveys. Secondary data includes information from community development groups, educational institutions, marketing consulting groups, and newspapers and magazines.

Budget concerns.–A strategy for image management can be expensive. Most churches plan at least 5 percent of their budgets for promotion. However, total image management may require as much as 10–12 percent of a church's budget.

Market for Uniqueness

Clarify the church's identity.–Primary and secondary data and entrance and exit interviews will help the committee refine the church's image. Ask questions to find out what the church is doing well–and what it is not doing well! If your church does not have a mission statement, now is the time to develop one. If it does, decide if it is accurate or if it is time for a new one.

Develop a "market niche."–Consider using a SWOTs approach to evaluate the church's identity. Honestly listing the churches strengths, weaknesses, opportunities, and threats will help the church find its best niche.

Develop Quality Communication Tools

Examine the church's newsletter, worship bulletin, letterhead, and other printed materials to see if they need to be updated.

Seek quality.–Provide the best quality you can afford.

Know your audience.–Get feedback from the congregation about the content of the newsletter and other publications. Make sure a first-time reader or visitor can understand the message offered.

Evaluate the Process

As actions are taken, watch for results and record the impact changes make. Watch for changes in knowledge about church activities and ministries, changes in attitude or opinion, growth in membership and/or attendance, changes in familiarity with the mission statement.

The process is ongoing. Ongoing image management will ensure that the church is consistently and positively known throughout your community.

Adapted from Bo Prosser, "Image Management," *Church Administration from A to Z* (Nashville: Convention Press, 1994), 129-53.

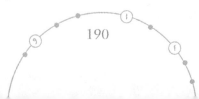

92. HOW TO Write Newspaper Ads That Get Results

A member of a pastor search committee once shared that she had first attended her church as a result of seeing a small newspaper ad telling of a seminar to be held at the church building. Now she is a vital part of her congregation. Though not everyone is drawn to a congregation in this manner, wise use of your newspaper advertising dollar may mean the difference between growth and stagnation.

But before placing an ad in the next edition of the local paper, first do a little homework. A quick phone call or visit to the local newspaper offices will help to establish rapport with the representative assigned to you. Find out as much as you can about the requirements of that particular newspaper regarding advertising.

Discover What financial Resources Might Be Available
Is it in the budget? Could newspaper advertising be included next year? Are there other funding sources?

Determine How Much the Ad Will Cost
Newspaper advertising can be expensive. Will you be running the ad on a regular basis? If so, you might discover that your newspaper has what is called "contract rates."

Your Ad Should Grab the Attention of the Reader
This is not easy if your ad looks like all the other ads on the page. Consider different type styles and innovative ad logos.

Most Churches Run Their Ads on Saturday
It may be better to place your ad on a day when fewer churches are running ads.

The So-called "Church Page" or Religion Section May Not Be the Best Place Either

Who would you like to reach with your ad? What part of the paper do they read most closely?

Your Ad Should Tell the Reader Something About Your Church

Include more information than your phone book ad contains. Let your ad be a reflection of the people in your church.

Develop and Use an Original Logo

The logo should be easily read and recognized.

Consider Using Photos and Testimonials of Church Members

Be sure to select individuals with exemplary Christian lives.

93. (HOW TO) Find and Enlist a Staff Member

Where are prospective staff members found? Many religious organizations and denominational offices have minister relations departments that assist churches with prospective workers. Calls can be made to friends and denominational workers in other areas to secure names of prospects. Encourage church members to share names of people who have impressed them. Churches should not hesitate to interview and call recent graduates who have prepared for ministry.

Once recommendations have been obtained and evaluated, it is essential that full information be secured for the most promising prospect(s). Some feel that the prospective staff member should be thoroughly investigated before any formal contact. Others prefer a conference call or an informal, get-acquainted visit in the home or office of the prospect. It seems best to have consent from the person before beginning any formal investigation.

In the contacts/conferences that follow, great care should be given in describing the church, the position, other staff members, the people, prospects for growth, and how the prospective staff member can aid the church. Discuss negative as well as positive factors related to the position and the church. If God leads the church and the prospect to each other, this honesty and openness will have long-term dividends. Don't rush the process until there is a strong consensus that God is leading.

Here are specific questions the prospective minister and the search committee should ask themselves in the evaluation process:

1. Does the prospect display leadership skills? Today's churches demand people who can lead.
2. Is an overwhelming sense of God's call evident in the prospect?
3. Is there a strong commitment to teach and preach God's Word?
4. Is the person flexible while remaining true to the Bible? "Rolling with the punches" seems to be a necessary trait of church leaders.
5. Is the prospective staff member a generalist? This trait is helpful in local churches. A staff member who is interested in and helpful toward all church programs is important.
6. Are there indicators of continued growth in the individual? Staff members need an ongoing program of education and updating of knowledge.

7. Is there an evident love for people and their needs? The staff member who stays secluded day after day will have a difficult time in relating to the real-life needs of people.

8. Is the person capable of being an example of character before the congregation?

After the committee members come to the conclusion that the prospect may be the person God would have in their church, they are ready to take the final step in the search process. This step is twofold.

First, the prospect must come to the same conclusion. There must be enough interest to make a visit, meet the people, and—along with the church—consider the possibility of an invitation to join the staff. After this has been done, the prospective staff member will need to seek God's will in the matter.

Second, church members should have an opportunity to meet the prospective staff member. The leaders with whom the staff member would have the most exposure should assuredly have dialogue with the prospect. The future effectiveness of the staff person can be harmed or enhanced by the way this get-acquainted visit is conducted.

At the conclusion of the visit, the church also will need to seek God's will and decide whether to invite the prospective minister to join the staff. If an invitation is extended, compensation according to the salary plan should be stated clearly to both church and future employee. There should be a general agreement as to the position expectations and performance standards. If the church approves and the staff member accepts, both parties then begin to establish the new partnership.

94. (HOW TO) Build Healthy Staff Relationships

Staff relationships are rewarding. They can also be frustrating. Attending to relationships can make all the difference. Answering the following questions can help a minister determine if he is attending to staff relationships.

Philosophy
• How do I view others' ministries in light of my own call from God?
• Do I operate from a shared or a solo ministry philosophy?
• Do I view other ministers as associates or assistants?
• Do I view members of the office and janitorial staff as vital elements of the work and life of the church, or do I view them as second-class citizens?

Authority
• Which management style dominates my leading of other ministers? Do I direct or dictate, coach or command?
• Do I have a top-down, autocratic management style or a negotiating style?
• How do I respond to the those who comment on my work?
• Are constructive critiques of ministry performance well received?

Success
• How do I deal with the popularity or success of another minister?

Equitable Compensation
• Are staff compensation packages an issue of concern?
• Do I have negative attitudes concerning the income of other ministers?
• Do those attitudes adversely affect relationships with certain staff members?

Communication
• Is the staff climate conducive to open and honest communication?
• Are any of these negative styles evident in my communication—placating, blaming, computing, or distracting?

Trust
• Can we trust one another with confidential matters?

Turf
• Are areas of ministry off limits to certain staff members?
• Do I consider any area of my work my personal territory?

Support
• Do the members of our ministry team support one another?
• Do we stand together when risks are taken and conflict occurs?

If these questions offer any warning signs, take these steps to improve staff relationships.

1. Start with a clear understanding of expectations, roles, and responsibilities.
2. Provide the opportunity for all staff members to take a personality profile.
3. When beginning a new relationship, anticipate difficulties and allow for a period of adjustment.
4. Establish a periodic review schedule to discuss perceptions of ministry performance.
5. Plan for fellowship.
6. Be a Barnabas; encourage your staff.
7. Pray for and with other staff members.
9. When a minister moves to serve on another church field, seek to maintain the relationship.

The rewards of building strong, healthy staff relationships are worth the efforts. Good staff relationships permeate the entire body. They model good relationships for the congregation and provide meaningful, lifetime friendships.

Adapted from A. Perry Hancock, "Building Healthy Staff Relations," *The Theological Educator*, Fall 1996, 33–39.

95. (HOW TO) Lead Your Staff to Be a Team

A team of people working cooperatively can produce more than the sum of individual members working alone. Why? Because of a phenomena called *synergy*. Individuals enhance one another's ideas and efforts through creative "hitchhiking." One good idea stimulates one in another team member, but only if they are working together toward a common goal and communicating regularly. Synergy is the secret of effective teamwork.

What Are the Requirements for Effective Teamwork?

1. The team needs committed, involved, visionary leadership. As pastor, learn to become an effective leader for your staff team.
2. The leader must be willing to examine his or her role in relation to the team. This often comes down to the personal style of a team leader meshing with the goals of the team and with his own vision of how best to reach those goals.
3. The team as a whole must adopt a strong sense of commitment and responsibility toward its common efforts.
4. The team must be willing to examine and critique its own performance, not just after a set time elapses but throughout the life of the team. This kind of self-examination can be done in a constructive, healthy manner.
5. The team must meet regularly as a whole. Any business transacted through a limited number of people tends to give those people more control than those who are not involved. This is faction-building and is ultimately very destructive. A church staff team should probably meet every week.
6. Teamwork should not end at the conference room door. The goals and processes of the team should become an integral part of each member's professional life.
7. As long as the team can justify its existence, its work is never finished. It should put itself through a continual process of diagnosis, action planning, implementation, and constant evaluation.

In *The Team Builder*, Frank Lewis suggested the following steps to help your church staff remain focused as a team.

Be a shepherd, not a shamer.—Be sensitive and gentle. The team member may be struggling with a feeling that God is leading in a new direction.

Exercise grace.—An unfocused team member may be facing some great challenge at home. An attitude of grace may open the door for you to minister to them in the future.

Provide the resources needed for professional counseling.—If a Christian counselor is needed by someone on your team, church insurance should provide some expenses for counseling. The team member may need assistance and be embarrassed to ask.

Be honest.—Team members may lack focus because of rumors in the church about upcoming change. Deal with these possibilities in an open and honest manner.

Be willing to "care-front" a team member when the time is right.—When a team member is involved in destructive behavior, offer help. Personal and caring intervention may be the answer. We expect much of team members, but they are only human.

Adapted from Philip G. Hanson and Bernard Lubin, "Team Building as Group Development," *Organization Development Journal.*

96. (HOW TO) Lead Your Staff as an Effective Supervisor

The effective supervisor is approachable.—He is interested in people and is concerned with their personal problems and growth. He seeks opportunities to help them solve problems and grow in usefulness. He values and protects confidences as privileged communication.

The effective supervisor is patient.—He tries to help and equip those who are struggling to become more effective Christian workers. He seeks to empathize with them and discover the necessary facts to help them solve their problems.

The effective supervisor is a good communicator.—He tries to speak on the level of his hearers. He seeks to speak intelligently and clearly concerning the area under discussion, and he tries to bring into the discussion the best of knowledge and resources available.

The effective supervisor maintains a sense of humor.—He can laugh at himself and with others and always appreciates a humorous story.

The effective supervisor has confidence in himself and in the people with whom he works.—He seeks to understand the problems that exist and tries to approach them with confidence and honesty.

The effective supervisor is a friend.—I know there are exceptions, but it is a great joy when pastor and staff team are also friends. He seeks to be a friend to all he is trying to help and to gain their confidence and understanding. He does not force himself on others but seeks through conferences and personal interviews to help those who would grow as leaders and as Christians.

The effective supervisor seeks to work with the persons supervised to develop a plan for meeting that person's needs and to help him develop to his fullest potential.—To help people maximize their potential, the leader-supervisor must take time to get to know each worker personally. Then training opportunities can be provided and encouraged to meet workers needs.

The effective supervisor holds team members accountable to carry out their ministries with excellence and dedication.—Weekly team meetings, job descriptions, and annual performance reviews are tools for accountability.

The effective supervisor must be an effective Christian in his daily life and in his witness to the lost.—How can you encourage workers to stay close to God if you do not include a daily quiet time in your schedule? This, of course, is a matter of personal integrity. Your workers may sense that your life is out of balance or that something is wrong, but they are not likely to know if you are failing to spend time alone with God. You will know, and your ministry will suffer. So maintain your devotional time, and encourage your workers to follow your example!

Resource
Holcomb, Tim. J., compiler. *Personnel Administration Guide for Southern Baptist Churches.* Nashville: Convention Press, 1988.

97. ⬤ HOW TO Terminate a Staff Member

Sometimes a staff member should be fired because of serious moral failure or ethical misconduct. Indeed, if a church finds out about misconduct of a staff member involving sexual misconduct in a counseling or child-care situation and does not remove the staff member from that position, the church can be liable for damages that might result from subsequent misconduct.

Dismissal may be appropriate when a staff member fails to fulfill job requirements; the church and the staff member are unable to work through critical differences; or the staff member's gifts, skills, and personality may prevent him from performing adequately at a particular church.

Distinguish between ministerial and nonministerial staff.—There may be distinctions between the right of a church to fire ministerial versus nonministerial staff members. Courts have granted churches more leeway in dismissing ministerial staff because of the spiritual aspects of their job.

Don't dismiss when the real problem is not the staff member.—The real problem may be a more powerful staff member, the personnel committee, or a select group of members who coerce and direct the dismissal decision for inappropriate reasons.

Find a Christian attorney in advance.—In any case involving dismissal of a key staff member, it is wise for the church to hire a Christian lawyer to review the facts and process before a dismissal situation is reached and the process completed.

Always conduct honest employee evaluations.—Each church needs to develop a job description for every employee. The job description should be broken down into a list of tasks, and performance expectations should be explained to each employee. If the job is not being done properly, the employee needs to be constructively trained about how to improve job performance.

Rules to Follow in Making a Dismissal Decision

1. Pay all wages and benefits to which the staff member is entitled in a timely manner.

2. Prior to disclosing highly charged information regarding a former staff member to a potential employer of that staff member, the disclosing church should ask for and have in hand a release from the former staff member authorizing the disclosing church to give facts in good faith and releasing the disclosing church from liability for damages which might be suffered from the disclosure of the information.

3. Do not mishandle the discharge in a way that attacks the dignity and privacy of the dismissed staff member.

4. Consider having contracts with staff members that protect the right of the church to fire at its discretion and that establish conditions and amounts of severance pay that might be offered to a dismissed staff member. Such decisions should be made in a calm moment when rational heads are in control.

5. Every church needs to give honest and accurate employee evaluations even for the pastor.

6. Review the bylaws, constitution, and policies to determine who has the power to make the decision to dismiss a staff member and see if the required procedure needs to be modified.

7. Fire staff members when there is obvious immorality. Failure to do so can lead to a civil lawsuit against the church and to the award of actual and punitive damages for repeated, subsequent misconduct.

8. Don't try to get rid of your problem staff members by giving them good references to get them hired by other churches.

Adapted from Steven Lewis, "When You Must Terminate–Legal Realities," *Church Administration* (December 1997), 29-31.

Resource

Holcomb, Tim. J., compiler. *Personnel Administration Guide for Southern Baptist Churches.* Nashville: Convention Press, 1988.

98. (HOW TO) Approach Recreation Ministry

Every church uses recreation. It may not be well organized, but all churches do it. Banquets, parties, fellowships, sports teams, church picnics, drama, camping, special celebrations are a part of the life of most churches. People enjoy and need this fellowship and activity. Churches that seek to meet these needs offer opportunities for social, mental, physical, emotional, and spiritual growth. A well-organized recreation ministry with a balanced program will offer opportunities for growth in all these areas to all ages. Doing this with a vision of reaching, teaching, and winning the lost requires kingdom thinking and planning.

A recreation ministry that reflects kingdom thinking will support and help the church carry out the Great Commission of "going unto all the world." Kingdom planning seeks to minister to all participants by creatively using the tools of crafts, socials, camping, sports, wellness/fitness, drama, music, and continuing education. As these tools are used wisely, opportunities arise for evangelism, discipleship, fellowship, ministry, and worship. This kind of kingdom thinking will result in numerical and spiritual growth along with the expansion of ministry opportunities and missions advance.

Because our culture is so leisure oriented, a well-organized recreation ministry will put a church on the cutting edge of touching people's lives in a nonthreatening way. Recreation has a way of capturing people's imaginations. If you capture a group's imagination, they will be open to listening to you. If they will listen to you, you have access to their minds. If you have their minds, you have a way to communicate to their hearts. If you have their hearts, you can introduce them to Christ.

The recreation ministry of a church must have a "Christ distinctive." Part of this distinctive is creating an atmosphere where ministry and fellowship can happen. Another part is the possibility of personal involvement. Recent cultural directions are showing us that an "intentionally evangelistic" recreation ministry can often take the lead in introducing people to the gospel of Jesus. Recreation is a tool to help the church achieve the Great Commission which will lead it to evangelize, disciple, minister, fellowship, and worship.

Biblical Guidelines

Honor God.—"Whatever you do, do all to the glory of God" (1 Cor. 10:31, NASB). "Discipline yourself for the purpose of Godliness" (1 Tim. 4:7, KJV).

Relate to the whole person.—"Jesus increased in wisdom and stature, and in favour with God and man" (Luke 2:52, KJV). "I pray God your whole spirit and soul and body be preserved blameless unto the coming of our Lord Jesus Christ" (1 Thes. 5:23, KJV).

Create happiness.—"A merry heart doeth good like a medicine" (Prov. 17:22).

Use talents.—"Neglect not the gift that is in thee" (1 Tim. 4:14, KJV). "I am come that they might have life, and that they might have it more abundantly" (John 10:10, KJV).

Develop the fellowship of the church.—"By this shall all men know that ye are my disciples, if you have love one to another" (John 13:35).

A right approach includes the right kind of enlistment process. You change a program to a ministry at the point of enlistment. You enlist a coach, and how many games you win may be the measure of success of the season. You enlist a person to minister through coaching, and changed lives will be the result. Enlist a ceramics teacher, and everyone will have pots to give for Christmas. Enlist someone to minister while teaching ceramics, and you'll still have pots—with the added dimension of ministry.

Recreation ministry can be of tremendous value to your church. The right approach will help pave the way for success.

By John Garner, manager, Design and Support, Church Ministry Leadership, LifeWay Church Resources, Nashville, Tennessee.

Resources

Miller, Mike. *Kingdom Leadership: A Call to Christ-Centered Leadership.* Nashville: Convention Press, 1996.

Recreation and Sports Ministry Newsletter is available monthly from LifeWay Church Resources. For more information or to order call 1-800-458-2772.

99. (HOW TO) Choose the Best Leadership Model for Recreation Ministry

As your church initiates a recreation ministry, the church should vote in conference to support recreation as a method of ministry to assist the church in accomplishing the Great Commission. This clears the way for the congregation to elect a committee, to designate budget funds for programming, and to publicize in church publications. Through the Church Ministry Leadership Team or other proper channels, a church staff member or layman can bring the recommendation to the church.

Various-sized churches with different staff situations must determine who is responsible for the administration of the recreation ministry. The three following scenarios relate to the full organization (staff member, committee, coordinators or lead teams, and volunteers). The scenarios suggest three ways the recreation ministry may be organized. There may be, and often is, a natural progression as a church grows from one scenario to the next.

Scenario A

In a smaller membership church, where the pastor is the only staff member, a layman may be asked to develop the recreation ministry. This "director" should have full responsibility for the recreation ministry. Communication with the pastor and Church Ministry Leadership Team is important during formative, implementation, and development stages. Good communication between the pastor and the director of recreation ministries will help ensure a clear focus and direction compatible with the other ministries of the church. This person should work with a recreation committee.

Scenario B

When a church adds a staff member after the pastor, recreation supervision and administration usually passes to that person. The staff member with recreation as one of many responsibilities may choose to continue the "director plan" as the pastor did. He will depend on a dedicated committee. The staff member may or may not attend committee meetings. Having multiple assignments, the staff minister must delegate some programming and authority for quality ministry in all areas to take place. Many churches with active programs (even with a gym, open only when programmed), work successfully with this arrangement.

Scenario C

The point at which a church should have a full-time recreation minister is when it has a comprehensive program and/or a complex "drop in anytime" facility. This person's role will be to orchestrate the ministry. He/she still should depend on the recreation ministry committee, volunteers, lead teams, and possibly paid staff, for successful ministry and operation.

The scriptural admonition of 1 Corinthians 14:40 says, "Let everything be done decently and in order." The order which allows everything to go smoothly in all directions at the same time is called "organization." It provides framework, stability, and direction. Every group has it, whether formal or informal. Good organization creates many arenas where many persons can serve God through the church. Organization also minimizes conflict, duplication, and waste. It involves:

- Enlisting–finding the right person for each job.
- Delegating–empowering people with responsibility and authority.
- Nurturing–growing people in a job.
- Trusting–letting them carry out the job.

Involvement in any part gives each person a feeling of ownership in the whole. This gives avenues of expression to many talents and meets varied needs of many individuals. This fulfills the body of Christ concept found in 1 Corinthians 12:12-31, where each part of the body has a distinctly different function. The overall effort of these individuals works together to accomplish the mission of the church.

By John Garner, director, Ministry Team Leadership Department, LifeWay Church Resources, Nashville, Tennessee.

100. (HOW TO) Develop a Leadership Team for Your Recreation Ministry

The church personnel committee, Church Council, or the pastor should designate the person with responsibility for the recreation ministry. Just as with any leadership position, with the responsibility should go the authority and budget support to do the job needed. The church in conference should approve this designation.

To be successful, it is necessary to develop a system for implementing, maintaining, and developing the recreation ministry. A recreation ministry committee should be chosen by the church. Draw together the best persons in your church to administer the recreation ministry. If a staff person will coordinate the ministry, that staff person should have major input into who is chosen for this assignment. These persons should:

- Be committed Christians.
- Be active church members.
- Have a ministry concept of recreation.
- Understand the inner workings of a church.
- Be dedicated to reaching and growing people for God.
- Have the necessary time.

The committee should be made up with diversity of interests. Members should not all be professionals or all sports oriented. They should represent several membership elements in the church. The committee will rotate just as other church committees do. It should meet regularly, at least quarterly, or monthly if needed.

The word *ministry* should be in the committee's name. This is important as it will help teach and communicate the intent of everything that is done. In too many cases, recreation is thought of as "extra" or peripheral.

Functions of the Recreation Ministry Committee

1. Advise the staff member with recreation responsibility or the recreation director.

2. Develop and protect the purpose, philosophy, theology, and policies for the recreation ministry. This should be approved by the Church Council and by the church in conference.

3. Enlist coordinators and lead teams to develop major areas of involvement and programming.

4. Receive and consolidate calendar dates, leadership enlistment, and budget recommendations from coordinators.

5. Be responsible for long-range planning.

6. See that recreation events are intentionally evangelistic with outreach to prospects and inreach to inactive church members.

7. Ensure that every aspect of church recreation:
   • Honors God
   • Is in harmony with the church's purpose.
   • Channels people into church program organizations and church membership.

8. Make personal growth available through self-improvement classes, leadership roles, and events that provide strengthened relationships.

9. Be vigilant to see that ministry is the purpose of the committee and program's existence.

10. Provide a balanced calendar to ensure that the ministry is well-rounded, functional, and not dominated by any person or program area.

11. Provide a proper atmosphere where ministry can happen.

12. Maintain facilities, maximize their use, and project needed improvements.

By John Garner, director, Ministry Team Leadership Department, LifeWay Church Resources, Nashville, Tennessee.

Resource

Recreation and Sports Ministry Newsletter is available monthly from LifeWay Church Resources. For more information or to order call 1-800-458-2772.